WILD
WATERS

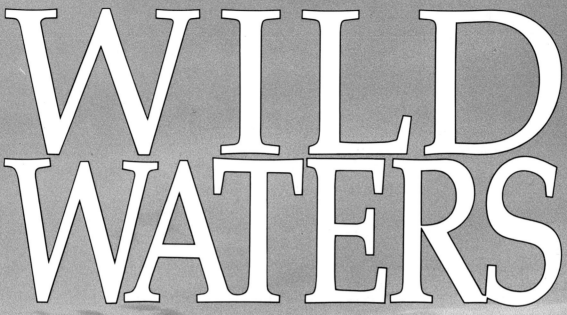

WILD WATERS

Canoeing Canada's Wilderness Rivers

EDITED BY JAMES RAFFAN
FOREWORD BY BILL MASON

KEY PORTER BOOKS

CANADIAN CATALOGUING IN PUBLICATION DATA

Main entry under title:

Wild waters : canoeing Canada's wilderness rivers

ISBN 0-919493-99-8

1. Canoes and canoeing — Canada.   2. Wild and scenic rivers — Canada.   3. Canada — Description and travel — 1981-   I. Raffan, James.

GV776.15.A2W55 1986   917.1'04647   C86-093929-4

Key Porter Books Limited
70 The Esplanade
Toronto, Ontario
Canada M5E 1R2

DESIGN: Brant Cowie/Artplus
COVER PHOTO: Alan Whatmough
MAP ART: Jack McMaster
TYPESETTING: Computer Composition of Canada, Inc.
Printed and bound in Italy

86 87 88 89   6 5 4 3 2 1

Page i: Wilberforce Falls — secret spectacle. Nearing Canada's northern coastline, the Hood River cascades 90 m in two steps to the floor of a red quartzite gorge. Named in 1821 by Sir John Franklin after British philanthropist, William Wilberforce, this remote cataract is thought to be the world's highest north of the Arctic Circle.

Pages ii–iii: Kazan Falls – a jewel of the Barrens.

Contents

ACKNOWLEDGEMENTS

To Michael Keating and Bill Mason, who channelled a trickle of ideas into the river of interest that became *Wild Waters*;

To biologists Bruce Lyon and Robert Montgomerie, who explained birds' nests along the way;

To friend and colleague R.H. Horwood, who, from the top of a nearby hill, found new hazards and patterns in the completed manuscript;

To Charis Wahl and Susan Renouf, who kept the book on course through production;

To those Mentors who taught us to see and to be swayed by the power of a river experience;

And to my wife and partner Gail Simmons, who, midstream in this book journey of which she was so much a part, delivered an 8 lb. 1 oz. bundle to join us on adventures to come;

Thank you all.

*To the native people who showed us
these rivers that we call wild*

Foreword

BY BILL MASON

In a lifetime of canoeing you couldn't paddle all the rivers of Canada. You could hardly paddle all the major rivers, let alone the thousands of obscure little wilderness rivers that have rarely seen a canoe. I get depressed just thinking about all those rivers that I will never see. One problem is that when I fall in love with a river, such as the Petawawa, the Puskaskwa or the Nahanni, I've got to see it again and again. I've actually worn a groove down the middle of the Petawawa I've run it so many times. I could spend a lifetime on the Nahanni and never satisfy my curiosity about all those feeder streams and the rivers that flow into it out of hidden valleys. I long to know what's up there. So what do you do? Even if you lived to a hundred you're not going to see even a fraction of them.

I've heard it said, "You see one river, you've seen them all." But that's like walking into the Louvre and saying, "You see one picture, you've seen them all!" Each river is a personality. A good contour map of a river is like a portrait. It gives you a picture of the temperament you can expect from it. Some rivers are young and boisterous, some old and rather grand in their bearing. Some rivers are totally unpredictable. They flow through so many types of terrain that you never know what to expect. There are rivers that will bore you one minute and kill you the next. It takes a while really to get to know them.

Half the fun of being a canoeist is sharing a river with friends. You can take them with you or tell them about it or show them your slides. I have had a glorious time sharing my love of rivers through films that I have made, and now I do it through painting. Books are probably one of the best ways to share a river because the reader can experience it again and again. With a book you have instant recall. I appreciate those who have shared their rivers with me: I feel as though I have caught a glimpse of that river's personality. Often it will convince me to go and see it for myself. Knowing what to expect can heighten the joy of anticipation that all canoeists experience before a trip.

There is always a fear that over-popularizing a river will destroy its wilderness character. This is a real and legitimate concern, for it has happened to many rivers. However, a natural outgrowth of falling in love with a river is a concern for its well being, its health and wild character. This in turn leads — or should lead — to one more voice speaking up for its preservation. I've always felt that a river is much more than a place to go to have fun. A river is a living being that can speak to the soul or the spirit. Wild rivers are an endangered species. They are being lost at an alarming rate, gobbled up by our industrial world. But we are not only physical beings: the spiritual part of us is just as important. I might never get to many or most of those rivers, but knowing they are out there, wild and free, fills me with anticipation and excitement.

This book is a means of sharing some of the rivers that have spoken to us. We hope they will speak to you.

I did not envy Jim Raffan's job of narrowing the selection to fit between these covers — this book should have been several feet thick — but I believe he has chosen well. I can think of no one better to set the guidelines for this book and to pull together the diversified talents of the canoeists found herein. Jim is a skilled white-water instructor, wilderness guide and expert on wilderness medicine. What impresses me most about Jim Raffan, though, is his concern for wild places and for the animals and plants that live there; and he has chosen writers who share his concern. We are only visitors, part of these wild places for a while. And we are so much richer for having been there, whether in person or in books such as this.

Overleaf: *Made golden by the yellow light of evening, tamarack trees in the Nahanni River's First Canyon stand out against forest and cliff. Dark spots on the canyon walls mark entrances to intriguing craters and caves in the porous limestone.*

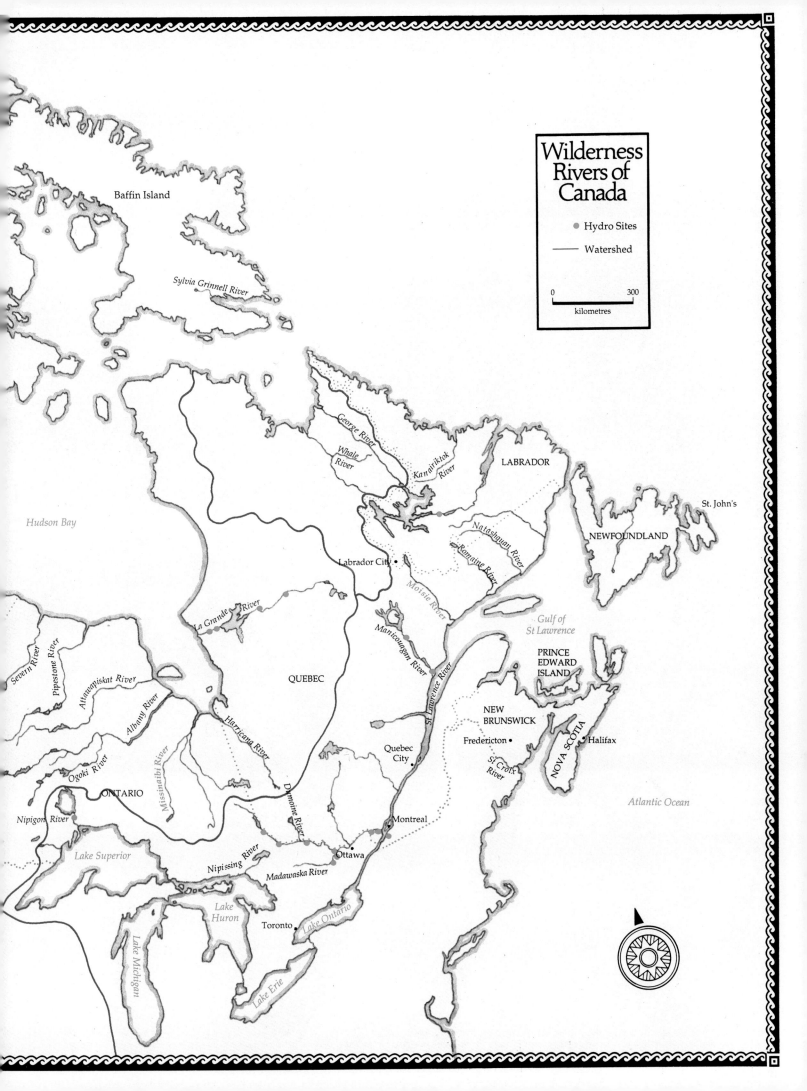

Wilderness Rivers of Canada

- Hydro Sites
- Watershed

0   300
kilometres

Baffin Island

Sylvia Grinnell River

George River

Whale River

Kanairiktok River

LABRADOR

St. John's

Natashquan River

NEWFOUNDLAND

Romaine River

Labrador City •

Moisie River

Hudson Bay

La Grande River

Manicouagan River

Gulf of
St Lawrence

Severn River

Pipestone River

Attawapiskat River

QUEBEC

PRINCE
EDWARD
ISLAND

Albany River

St Lawrence River

Harricana River

NEW
BRUNSWICK

Ogoki River

Missinaibi River

Fredericton •

Halifax

ONTARIO

St Croix River

NOVA SCOTIA

Nipigon River

Dumoine River

Quebec
City

Atlantic Ocean

Lake Superior

Montreal

Nipissing River

Ottawa

Madawaska River

Lake
Huron

Toronto •

Lake Ontario

Lake Michigan

Lake Erie

International River Classification Scale

Reference is made in this volume to the International River Classification Scale, which is used by white-water paddlers to categorize rapid difficulty.

I	Moving water with a few riffles and small waves; no obstructions.
II	Easy rapids with waves up to one metre. Channels are wide and obvious without scouting. Some manoeuvring necessary.
III	Rapids with high, irregular waves that could swamp an open canoe. Narrow passages require scouting and complex manoeuvring.
IV	Long and difficult rapids with constricted passages that often require precise manoeuvring in turbulent water. Scouting from shore is often necessary and conditions make rescue difficult. Generally impossible for open canoes.
V	Extremely difficult, long, and very violent rapids. Complicated routes must be scouted from shore. Significant hazard to life in event of mishap.
VI	Difficulties of Class V carried to the extreme of navigability. Nearly impossible and very dangerous for closed canoes. Serious risk to life.

It is accepted practice to consider rapids one class more difficult in cold or extreme-wilderness conditions. This scale is for paddler reference only. Ratings change with river water levels.

Wild river canoeing — passport to a Canadian dream. In insect country, a repellent-soaked bug jacket or "citronella negligée" is a must, especially when winds are calm.

CHAPTER ONE

OUR WILD RIVERS

This book is a celebration of Canada's wild rivers. It features eight expedition-length rivers, which encompass the rich diversity of Canada's wild-river heritage. The rivers were selected not because they are wilder or more scenic or cleaner than wilderness water courses close to home, but in order to permit a number of seasoned wilderness travellers to share their distinctive ways of valuing the river experience. From the rain-washed Moisie in the east to the turbid Bonnet Plume in the west, come experience adventures on remote and dangerous rivers, some protected, others not, and one – the Liard – now collared and leashed for good. But first, explore the quintessential Canadian river experience and see that these wild rivers are a diminishing resource whose continued existence will not come without the work and commitment of Canadians from every part of the country.

Wild But Not Free

BY JAMES RAFFAN

It saddens me that the wild-river valley where I grew up is now under water. In truth, the Speed River north of Guelph, Ontario — "the mighty Speed" we called it — was no more wild than your average Holstein. But along its banks, in a riverside corridor where farmers couldn't plow, willows hung over fish-twitching pools, and tangled thickets made a boy's wilderness.

With an unquenchable spirit of adventure, I'd wander up the river to places that nobody else knew about, past the spot where a flood-control dam now squats, and into territory that, I was sure, was just short of the North Pole. Using logs and bits of wood ripped loose by spring ice, I'd build a raft and drift home, late for supper and usually very wet. I was Christopher Columbus, Huck Finn, Captain Hook, and Guy the Voyageur. Or just a kid, wondering who fed the ducks and where the water came from.

The rafts were replaced by summer-camp canoes and my life expanded to include other streams and other adventures. I'm sure that nothing has had greater effect on my view of the world than a long succession of river expeditions that began so simply, so close to home. Surviving wild northern waters and harsh weather bred self-reliance. Being swayed by the power of swollen rivers and wilderness led to my feeling comfortable separate from the trappings of home. The stories, memories, and river-deep friendships that grew out of these experiences have richly colored my life.

But shortly after graduating from university in biology, an arctic river reopened my eyes. Standing on the barren shores of the Coppermine River, overwhelmed by black-flies and mosquitoes, I felt, for the first time, like a visitor in a river world. Fear of a forbidding place forced me to attend to the river in a way I had never done before. It taught me that fish don't need fish ladders if there are no dams. It taught me that human emotion confounds our understanding of the relationship of wolf and caribou. And it taught me that without barriers, only caution prevents slipping over the brink. I learned what wild really means.

With a head crammed with scientific exactitudes, it took the Coppermine River community to show me that nature does not revolve around human interests. I saw budding horns of a uniquely human dilemma: I

The real joy of river travel comes from exploring the total river environment. On the Coppermine River, "Rocknest," a prominent hill near its source gives a remarkable overview of the mighty river.

Coppermine white water — a test of team work and skill. The removable spray cover widens safety margins in rough, cold (8°C) northern waters. Caribou antlers on board make an awkward yet memorable souvenir.

was awed by things wild, yet I knew that just by being there I interrupted the flow of nature. I had to conclude that the only meaningful way to view the world was not through my own eyes but from some distant hill, seeing myself as just one element in a much larger scheme. I also saw the canoe as the perfect vehicle for a peaceful resolution of the dilemma. In it I could be part of nature.

At the same time I made new connections to history. Around quiet campfires on the Coppermine, smoke from gnarled wood tweaked our imaginations as we talked of native people and read from the journals of Samuel Hearne and Sir John Franklin. Like never before I felt part of our Canadian past. I realized that the river routes that reticulate this land from sea to arctic sea bear the very essence of who we are. By paddling the Coppermine, stripped of school and its interpreters, I was experiencing the land much as Hearne, Franklin, and its native custodians had left it centuries earlier. Reason enough, I thought, to treasure the river.

Indeed, many lives have been changed, for better and for worse, by capricious northern waters. River adventures give us new eyes, new ways of looking at the world, sometimes immediate, sometimes latent, and often in a transferable, metaphorical way. John Kauffman has contemplated the "mysterious element to the ever-changing changelessness of flowing water. Rivers prompt us to ask where from, where to, how deep, and what is around the bend?" In 1909, Agnes Laut wrote, "It is a curious sensation, canoeing down a vast river whose waters sweep an area equal to half a dozen European kingdoms and at every bend reveal shifting vistas of new peoples and new regions." Contributing author Bob Henderson speaks of a "strange freedom surfaced in this primitive setting, in activity, materials, and desire linked so closely with the land." And back-country philosopher Willi Unsoeld described the meaning of a wilderness experience as "a renewal exercise that leads to a process of alteration. You go to nature for your metaphysical fix — your reassurance that the world makes sense. It's a reassurance that there's something behind it all and it's good."

There are those to whom metaphysical notions are as foreign as travelling the same route twice. They crash down northern streams just to collect river names like so many stuffed lion heads. "River baggers," as they've been called, miss the real river experience.

Other paddlers would keep wild rivers secret. Yet, the "ever-changing changelessness" of a river, which makes *every* river experience

unique, and gives people this desire to keep secrets, is the same trait that allows paddlers to be explorers again and again, discovering the invisible trails of their predecessors and leaving no tracks.

There are still others, bureaucrats who relate to rivers through statistics. They insist that rivers of cultural or ecological significance should be catalogued, rivers of big vertical drop and constant flow should be dammed, and urban rivers should be used to dilute wastes to acceptable levels.

We all have our favourite river close to home, but more and more expedition-quality wild rivers now figure in the designs of paddlers, rafters, politicians, and technocrats. This leaves me naggingly questioning why the existence of these priceless communities must be rationalized in the human context. Why must wild rivers justify their undammed, undeveloped state? Is it too much to ask that a river be left alone for its own sake?

Unfortunately, the answer is yes. In countless head-to-head battles between economics and ecology, rivers have lost. In the human world, in which the laws of economics overrule laws of nature, we may have to put barriers around the precious parts of our river heritage to even the odds.

If we do so, we should acknowledge three things. We must recognize that parks in themselves are paradoxical: protective barriers mean increased use. Second, because such barriers tend to constrict the natural evolution of a river, we must enclose tracts of land large enough to allow the river community — not the park — to dominate. And most important, we must acknowledge that recreational, commercial, and government river users must co-operate! The alternative is the Ottawa River, voyageur highway to the west. Once wild, it will not be wild again, at least not in this ice age.

We know how to live in harmony with nature: we can clean water before we put it back in the rivers; we can tap and process mineral resources without scarring the landscape; and we can utilize natural power sources without compromising every river valley in the country. But whether what we *can* do becomes what we *will* do is largely dependent on how many people adopt a new way of looking at our rivers.

This view may mean that boaters will have to stand in line for the

Evening camp: mirrored images of tree and cloud play on still waters while a tired crew reflects on a rich river day. It's time for setting up tents, preparing a fireside supper and reliving the day's highlights.

privilege of paddling popular wild rivers. It may mean that regulated promotion of increased river use will be seen as a necessary and useful trade-off for increased awareness, appreciation, and advocacy; because there is no substitute for actually having been *on* a wild river when it comes to speaking up for preservation. It may mean ecologists and industrialists will have to focus on their similarities and not on their indignations. A new river view may mean that we will have to issue permits for river use, as the Americans do.

The major rivers in our primary drainage basins — Columbia in the Pacific, Mackenzie in the Arctic, Nelson flowing to Hudson Bay, and St. Lawrence in the Atlantic basin — are heavily exploited, and development schemes metastasize. Inhospitable geography has protected most of our wild rivers and will probably continue to do so, because travel is difficult in the mountains and high on the Canadian Shield. Yet it is increasingly possible to manage large tracts of river land by remote control. Witness the Churchill River in Labrador and the La Grande in Quebec: beyond civilization, we thought, but today they are dammed and silent.

In the 1930s Thomas W. Kierans came up with an idea to create a sea-level, dike-enclosed freshwater lake within James Bay from which water would be channelled to southern markets. His proposal still gets attention. Protecting our wild rivers from such maniacal schemes might best be done through legislated wilderness, a profound contradiction. It makes sense to cordon off significant wild areas, and it's naïve to think that anything less will have lasting effect. If one day a united consciousness narrows the gap between environmental understanding and environmental degradation we can take the fences down; meanwhile, we need laws to keep our wild rivers wild.

The Americans passed the Wild and Scenic Rivers Act in 1968; and we recently established the Canadian Heritage Rivers System, an initiative involving all levels of government in the protection of our valuable rivers. Under the system, our rivers are evaluated on their merits, not solely on whether they advance human development plans. It's a big step in the right direction, and the scheme just might work!

Rivers are at the very heart of this nation. Without them, who would we be? We must preserve them, and to do that we must take effective,

united — and informed — action. At stake is an irreplaceable treasure that is very much a part of who we are. In *Why We Act Like Canadians* Pierre Berton put it this way:

> . . . *we are a nation of canoeists, and have been since the earliest days, paddling our way up the St. Lawrence, across the lakes, over the portages of the Shield, west along the North Saskatchewan through the Yellowhead gap and thence southwest by the Columbia and Fraser rivers to the sea. When somebody asks you how Canada could exist as a horizontal country with its plains and mountains running vertically, tell him about the paddlers.*

And while you're at it, like the authors of the following fine river tales — Mason, Franks, Henderson, Harrison, Schaber, Gaskin, Pelly, and York — tell him about the rivers, the wild rivers of Canada.

The quality of light is one of the most compelling features of the northern landscape. Below, canoeists paddle into shimmering water under rapidly lowering skies; at bottom, canoes glide *silently through still water under a midnight sun; and, below right, the sun's rays draw water into the clouds from the deserted lake.*

Wild river cliffs provide important nesting habitat for large carnivorous birds. Viewed in early August from a photographer's makeshift blind, this fledgling Golden Eagle on the Coppermine River must learn to fly and hunt in the few weeks before the snow flies.

Racing to the Gulf of St Lawrence in a deep glacial valley through the rugged eastern edge of the Canadian Shield, the Moisie River is one of eastern Canada's most spectacular and challenging for canoeists.

CHAPTER TWO

EASTERN WILD

The eastern edge of the Canadian Shield is a forbidding wilderness, but through the centuries this land of deep river valleys, rain, and mosquitoes has engendered a strange fascination in the adventuresome few. Winter and summer, rugged individuals are drawn to such rivers as the George, Wheeler, and Whale, which flow into Ungava Bay; the Ugjoktok, Churchill, and Kanairiktok, which run through Labrador to the Atlantic; and the Little Mecatina, Natashquan, and Romaine, which flow from the highlands of Labrador to Quebec's North Shore. Perhaps the best known and most travelled eastern river, the one of greatest volume on the North Shore, is the Moisie. It rises in Lake Opocopa near the Labrador border and flows 420 kilometres south to the Gulf of St Lawrence near Sept-Iles, Quebec.

Moisie : Nahanni of the East

BY FRED GASKIN

Four modern-day voyageurs arrive in Labrador City with paddles, packs, and provisions for a two-week descent of Moisie River. All components for the expedition are accounted for except the two canoes which, having arrived in advance, are locked up in a warehouse, location unknown! It is also Regatta Day, a festival of summer games when the only signs of life were at the airport and the local bar. Our sole option is to leave the airport and begin our canoe search at the hotel.

The sympathetic woman bartender and local patrons systematically eliminate all storage possibilities until a phone call produces information as to the likely whereabouts of the local freight manager. He found the canoes in a locked warehouse within sight of the pre-trip watering hole. Kit complete, it is now possible to arrange our transport into the Labrador wilderness.

The Moisie, known to the Montagnais Indians as the "Mis-te-shipu," or Great River, is most often approached by crossing the height of land from Labrador. We had paddled together on many journeys in northern Ontario, the Northwest Territories, and western Quebec, but Ingo Schoppel, Robbert Hartog, Jack Purchase, and I were looking forward to our first major Quebec/Labrador wilderness river.

Unfortunately, we acted on poor advice and flew from Sept-Iles to Labrador City, thereby missing the opportunity of travelling north on the legendary Quebec North Shore and Labrador Railway. While trying to locate our errant canoes, we learned at the bar that despite reduced iron-mining operations in the interior, the QNS&L remains the best — and cheapest — way to gain access to the Moisie. It would have been a great ground-level preview of the Moisie lands.

So we wouldn't be totally deprived of rail transport, we rode the late evening "Cottage Run," west from Labrador City to our put-in on Lac De Mille, thirty kilometres east of town. We had our own boxcar for canoes and gear and spent the hour as guests of the trainmen in the locomotive. These would prove the most relaxing thirty kilometres of our two-week trip.

At 11:00 P.M. the train stopped, we bade farewell to our generous hosts, and paddled to an island where we set up camp — a camp that became home for two and a half days while heavy winds whipped the

Senses tingle to the fresh, damp smell of morning mist.

16

Early in its tempestuous run to the sea, the Moisie is joined by the Pekans River at this foaming confluence. The Pekans drops 140 m in the 10 km immediately upstream from the Moisie.

Two members of author Gaskin's crew line a loaded canoe through a side channel on the Moisie. The risk of the canoe upsetting and being lost downriver makes team work as important in this river manoeuvre as it is in paddling white water.

Running the rapids gives canoeists the ultimate sensation of exhilaration and achievement.

*The danger of spilling makes
flotation devices mandatory.*

lake. Fortunately, the weather moderated sufficiently by noon of the third day to permit us to cross Lac De Mille and ascend a creek to the portage over the height of land that took us into Quebec and to the headwaters of the Moisie River. We camped in an area devastated by forest fire and, it seemed, prone to natural disasters: we were sent rushing for the shelter of the tent after supper that night by a shower of marble-sized hailstones.

The following day, we were somewhat tense as we paddled across Lac Menistouc and Lac Opocopa and entered the Moisie. From here we would descend 420 kilometres to the gulf, running and portaging each day's ration of the challenging rapids we had heard so much about.

In addition to topographic maps, we had excellent information from "Gens Du Nord" of Sept-Iles to help us through the rapids. From experience with other such notes we knew that changing water levels tend to make these descriptions notoriously unreliable. Yet their annotated trip maps were flawless, and their rapid classifications on the international white-water scale were completely accurate. We concluded that the water levels in the year the notes were made were identical to ours in 1983. The notes were in French, but once we related the word *cordelle* to the process of lining, they saved us time and contributed to our success in completing the trip without a single upset.

No written description, however, can replace paddling expertise, experience, and good equipment. We had two 5.5-metre Old Town ABS voyageur canoes complete with deck covers, and were able to handle all Class III rapids with comparative safety. In conjunction with the Gens Du Nord maps, we defined Class IV rapids as having a "30% chance of upset," and Class V as "upset inevitable." Spray covers or not, we portaged many times a day, day after day!

The lower part of our descent of the Moisie River would retrace the historic canoe route of Henry Youle Hind who, in 1861, became the first European to explore this part of Quebec and Labrador. We had with us a copy of Hind's journal, which gave us opportunities to compare experiences of the rapids and canyons of the lower Moisie.

Our objectives were challenge, adventure, and recreation; but Hind, a professor of geology at the University of Toronto, was intent on mapping the Moisie and exploring the interior, in the hope of giving Labrador a place in the future of British North America. He had with him five French Canadian voyageurs, two Indian guides, two government surveyors, and his brother William, who went along as expedition artist (a usual requirement until the advent of the camera). On June 10,

*An evening paddle — alone with
still water, setting sun and an
empty canoe that seems to enjoy
a load-free frolic.*

Moisie rapids present a great variety of challenges for white-water paddlers. Depending on a group's skill, most river sections can be run; others should be lined or portaged. The relatively uniform gradient of the Moisie makes it one of the greatest sources for Atlantic salmon. For waterfowl, however, the swift current makes the Moisie an unpopular river for raising young.

Below: *Rain and mist continually haunt the Moisie River.*

1861, they began struggling upstream on the Moisie River against a current still swollen with spring run-off; they returned, one month later, whisked south by the many rapids of the Moisie.

We got many a taste of what Hind was up against. Halfway down one rapid, I spotted a portage. Ingo and I quickly stopped our descent, walked the canoe across ledges and rocks, and pulled into a well-used trail. Realizing that the portage was worn for good reason, we grabbed loose ropes and ran along the shore to provide whatever assistance we could to Robbert and Jack, who had missed the turn.

They were lodged on the rocks on the wrong side of the river just above a place where it dropped almost thirty metres straight down through a succession of falls. Careful upstream tracking and a tenuous river crossing reunited our party for the two-kilometre canyon portage. Frequent shore vantage points provided ample opportunity to appreciate and photograph the awesome beauty of the canyon and its crushing white water. We had often been told about spectacular white-water canoeing in Quebec and Labrador: without question, the Moisie upholds this reputation!

Another major portage took us to the massive cascades at the confluence of the Pekans River and the Moisie. The lively white water at the foot of the falls provided Ingo with six speckled trout in short order. In addition to the speckles, the frying pans contained sliced mushrooms, collected along the portage. Lunch, that day, was off the land.

Some canoeists use the Pekans River to approach the Moisie. This trip begins with road rather than rail transport out of Labrador City, but the proportion of portaging to canoeing on the Pekans is far greater, and its arrival at the Moisie is heralded by a three-kilometre portage. As we feasted on fresh trout and mushrooms, we studied the Pekans and concluded that our route was amply tough to satisfy our sense of adventure.

All the portaging and the possibility of severe weather forced us to spend long hours on the river to ensure that we would make it to Sept-Iles on the Labour Day weekend, within our two-week time limit. But this eight-to-nine-hour-a-day paddling schedule was suspended without hesitation on what was to be our only rain-free day of the entire journey. It was one of those warm, sunny days typical of northern Ontario river trips. We discovered a short but beautiful cascade broken by large rock islands spanning the river. We camped early in glorious sunshine and took a long-awaited and highly enjoyable rest.

Kitchen with a view.

Overleaf: *Dense forest
vegetation along the Moisie is
predominantly white and black
spruce, balsam fir, white birch,
trembling aspen and a few jack
pine. The only easy way to see
the valley is to hike up inflowing
streams such as this one.*

Robbert took on the duties of innkeeper and commenced preparations for a gourmet wilderness dinner, while Ingo endeavoured to fulfil a promise to provide speckled trout *hors d'oeuvres*. Jack and I set out to capture the beauty of the site on film and to prove it is possible to have a bath in the Moisie's icy water.

On our rock-island home, we found many scour holes — perfectly cylindrical cavities in the rock worn smooth by ice and water — as deep as a man and two metres wide. So intent were we in our inspection of this phenomenon that I fell into a hole hidden by foliage. Numerous scrapes, but thankfully no broken bones! With assistance from Jack, I limped back to camp in time for supper. The arrival of a crippled colleague evoked no sympathy, just concern that three able-bodied voyageurs were being set up to do the portaging for four!

A bad leg didn't preclude paddling and enjoying this canyoned river some call "the Nahanni of the east." It was exciting to hold back and watch Jack and Robbert proceed through the turbulence with an unerring instinct, disappearing in the trough and returning to view farther on, all with optimum daring, tempered with an equivalent measure of safety. Our own descent would follow, retracing the route of the lead canoe or charting a new course, but with the same sensation of exhilaration and achievement.

At one point, the river narrowed to a dark ten-metre gap and drove through a short canyon. Deathly silent black water coursed between the rock walls, its smoothness broken only by miniature whirlpools that erupted and vanished. It was a strange and mystical sensation drifting through the canyon on a river unexpectedly silent, only a fraction of its normal width, but possibly a hundred times its usual depth.

Periodically the slopes of the river valley were punctuated with sparkling streams that cascaded hundreds of metres from the valley crest. They seemed to swell with every passing day.

To our chagrin, intermittent daily rains turned into a continuous downpour that seemed to last for days. We broke camp in the rain, portaged and paddled in the rain, ate lunch in the rain, and, paddling, looked in vain — in the rain — for our next campsite.

The low point of the trip was at eight o'clock on the evening we arrived at Fish Ladder portage, a grotty spot that would have to be home for four rain-soaked, chilled paddlers. There was barely adequate space for the tent. The temperature was falling toward freezing; and Ingo's uncontrollable shaking underlined the urgency of providing shelter,

Although summer temperatures are a comfortable 13-16°C, fog and drizzle occur frequently in the Moisie valley. In July and August, monthly precipitation averages around 9 cm, with measurable rainfall occurring on about 40% of summer days. Lack of campsites in the dense, wet forest forces tenters onto riverside rock, where the ground is flat and bugs are fewer.

fire, and warm, dry clothes. It was a frightening reminder of our fallibility. Two hours later, with spirits restored, we drank a rum toast to our arrival and survival.

When the sun's welcome rays penetrated the water-soaked forest, I was overwhelmed by one benefit of all this moisture. There were luxuriant mosses everywhere, as much as a metre deep, which have built up over the years; moss so thick that very little undergrowth develops in the northern Quebec rain forest. This moss made me appreciate rain, for the only time on the trip.

While paddling down the lower Moisie wilderness, we frequently noted evidence of three important Quebec resources: a salmon fishing lodge; the iron-ore trains of the QNS&L railway along the river; and in the far distance, hydro towers crossing the horizons with power for rural and urban communities.

This gradual return to civilization retraced Hind's homeward journey on the Moisie. It was at Hind's "fifth rapid" (second from the mouth of the Moisie River) that we decided to end our trip. Rather than run the rapid and risk a "50% chance of an upset," and to shorten the trip by twenty-five kilometres, we pulled out at the QNS&L railway bridge over the Moisie. Hind was right when he described "a steep and slippery mountain path — straight up!" It was quite a climb to get away from the river; fortunately, all our portaging had prepared us.

There was no one at the railway maintenance building and no telephone; however, we were fortunate to encounter one of the locals, who offered to take Robbert into town on his dirt bike to arrange for collecting our station wagon. Awaiting his return, as dusk was falling, three fatigued but contented voyageurs watched an ore train cross the bridge and disappear into a tunnel on its way to Sept-Iles. Like us, it was full of the riches of the north, and destined for the south.

Fred Gaskin's lifetime list of river expeditions reads like a gazetteer of Canadian wild waterways: Mackenzie, Hanbury/Thelon, Back, Kazan, Dubawnt, Harricanaw, Yellowknife/Coppermine, Burnside, Hood, Attawa piskat Winisk, Nahanni, and, of course, the Moisie, to mention only a few. He is a fellow of both the Explorers Club and the Royal Geographical Society based in London, England. Gaskin is a collector of rare books about arctic exploration and lives in Cambridge, Ontario, where he is president of Bradley, Gaskin, and Marshall insurance brokers.

A solo paddler rests in a quiet Missinaibi pool.

CHAPTER THREE

CENTRAL WILD

Because James Bay's great rivers are close to large centres of population, many have been dammed for power generation. But long before rivers such as the Mattagami, Abitibi, and La Grande were dammed, they provided an essential link between the fur-rich interior of central Canada and tidewater trading posts on James Bay. Fortunately, rivers such as the Harricanaw, Albany, and Attawapiskat remain much as they were centuries ago, when native paddlers and voyageurs used them to transport goods.

Missinaibi : After the Voyageurs

BY SARA HARRISON

Imagine embarking on a historic river journey that takes you northward from Lake Superior, over a height of land and down the Missinaibi, 426 unimpeded kilometres to James Bay. It is a sublime and spectacular encounter with a river that has a colourful heritage and an unusual diversity of geologic forms, plants, animals, and bird life. Undiminished in its wilderness character, the Missinaibi remains the only major river in northeastern Ontario that flows freely to James Bay.

It was in anticipation of such a journey that fellow Canadian Outward Bound Wilderness School instructor, Louis Barrette, and I chose the Michipicoten/Missinaibi route for an instructional canoe trip in the spring of 1981. In late May eight of us gathered on Lake Superior at the mouth of the Michipicoten River: two leaders and six participants from across Canada and as far away as Japan at the beginning of a twenty-eight-day river learning experience. For a day and a half we practised canoe-rescue techniques, flatwater paddling strokes, and first-aid skills, new friends learning to rely on one another for safety and mutual support.

For Louis and me, instructing a river course was a new experience. We would require a focus different from that of our many personal canoe trips. We would have to help our participants learn to read the river, to assess its dangers, and to manoeuvre skilfully its ever-changing features. Our goal was to instil a respect for the power of moving water, and to help develop the skills and judgment needed to paddle a remote river safely, thereby enhancing the participants' enjoyment of its challenges. High springtime water levels and cold temperatures would leave little margin for error.

We left behind the cries of herring gulls over Lake Superior and started up the Michipicoten River toward the edge of the Atlantic watershed. Most canoeists opt to drive to the village of Missanabi, avoiding the three hydro-electric power dams along this 100 kilometres of the historic fur trade route. We wanted to experience the route Indians and voyageurs had travelled; dams or no dams, covering the whole route was important.

The group adapted quickly to the daily schedules of the trail and began to work out a balance between self-reliance and interdepen-

The Michipicoten-Missinaibi-Moose rivers route was once an important fur-trade artery connecting James Bay to Lake Superior. From inland posts, furs worth fortunes were carried over portages around many rapids and falls en route to European markets. Through the din of rushing water, you can sometimes hear the ghostly shouts of the fur-brigade paddlers who walked these trails and played these wild waters.

Previous pages: *Split Rock Falls
— 5 km below St. Peter's Rapids
and 10 km upstream from St.
Paul's Portage.*

dence. Reaching Dog Lake, headwaters of the Michipicoten, we stopped to pick up a cache of supplies at the village of Missanabi and set out in search of the portage over the height of land between the Atlantic and Hudson Bay watersheds.

Crossing a major height of land was a big event for the voyageurs; yet, we were surprised by how nondescript this portage turned out to be. As we carried our gear along a very ordinary trail, it didn't feel like we were crossing a great divide, but we were thankful not to be portaging around another hydro-electric power dam, and appreciative of the Missinaibi's wilderness character. It is a river valley almost unchanged in appearance since the Ojibwa, Cree, and voyageurs utilized it as a main travel route.

When we finished the short portage, we faced Missinaibi Lake's notorious winds, kicking up ferocious waves. Undaunted, we danced polkas and jigs to stay warm, while we waited for the wind to abate. Back on the water we headed over to Fairy Point, a thirty-five-metre rock face covered with remarkable paintings.

"Missinaibi" is an Ojibwa word that roughly means "pictures on water" or "painted pictograph." It is an apt name, because there are many sites like Fairy Point along the river. No one is certain how old the sites are, exactly who painted the images, or what part they played in native culture. As we looked up at the cliff face from our canoes, the red ochre designs were a delight to the eye, quiet testimony of a way of life now vanished. Images of fish, caribou, and canoes reflected the intimate connection with the earth the native people had once known.

This encounter helped settle us into the rhythms of wilderness travel, its isolation, its silences. No longer were our senses subconsciously filtering information from the world around us; instead they began to soak it all in. Slowing down allowed us to see the world with a fresh perspective, less distracted, more attentive to the exquisite detail of the natural beauty all around us.

Much of what pulls me back to the Shield country is this timelessness and deep sense of familiarity. Paddling on a glacier-formed lake and hearing the call of a loon across the water, I felt like I had come home. This, I think, is what I was trying to share with our students.

At the northeast end of Missinaibi Lake we stopped at the site of an old inland trading post. Originally named Missinaibi Lake House, it was the second inland post of the Hudson Bay Company, built in 1777. Walking around this site, we talked of the rivalry between the North

"Snapper" — beady-eyed denizen of southern Canada. These large freshwater turtles are omnivorous, eating aquatic invertebrates, fish, reptiles, birds, mammals, carrion, vegetation and the occasional unwary canoeist.

Great Grey Owl — a rare find on the Missinaibi. In recent times, these magnificent birds have been sighted far south of their typical range, passing, on this occasion, through the valley of the Missinaibi.

West Company and the Hudson's Bay Company and how, unfortunately, it was often times the Indians who lost out in the fierce competition between the two. It was not hard to imagine brigades of lean, spry men and their *bourgeois* arriving, exchanging goods, tall tales, new songs, and gossip, and planning careful strategies for trade.

The Missinaibi River has a turbulent start at Quittagene Rapids. They were too high for us to run, so we portaged and took advantage of the swift run-out below to practise upstream ferries, eddy turns, and peelouts. It was an ideal place to get a feel for the power of the current, and each team strove to combine the right leans with the right strokes.

The next morning, we awoke to a light dusting of snow, a startling — albeit beautiful — reminder that it was still early in the year and the river was fast, and very cold. Not great for dumping.

Our confidence grew as we made our way down the river, lining, shooting, or portaging numerous rapids each day. We took time to allow each canoe team to consider what approach they would take with each rapids. This was a time-consuming, wet, and, at times, frustrating process; but Louis and I felt it was at the heart of learning how to make good river judgments. The hardest part was setting limits when we felt the participants' enthusiasm outmatched their white-water skills.

The river flows under the main line of the Canadian Pacific Railway just south of Peterbell Lake and changes from an enclosed water course full of rapids, with banks heavily lined with cedar trees, to a river that meanders through a flat, open string bog. One morning, I got up early and savoured the crispness of a new spring day on this part of the river. It was a chance for a little uninterrupted journal writing:

An early morning mist
lifts off the river
pink salmon clouds
announce the daybreak

frozen mitts
hang with icy tips
waiting for the start of day.

But the upper Missinaibi leaves little time for reflection: Deadwood Rapids, Split Rock Falls, St. Peter's Portage kept us busy. Getting behind schedule, we opted to portage without scouting rapids for a while. This was quicker, but not nearly as satisfying.

Sometimes, however, we would slow down, tie the canoes together, and have a leisurely lunch rafting down the river, laughing, talking, and letting distance roll by. Other times we would camp early. With thoughts of safety and river running behind us for the day, we would fish and bake, and savour the Shield country, often drifting off to sleep to the sound of rapids rising and falling.

The Trans-Canada Highway crosses the river at the French-speaking community of Mattice, west of Cochrane. That this would be the only place where we would encounter civilization brightened my soul. We quickly replenished our dwindling baking supplies, bought some fresh vegetables, picked up our mail, and continued on. We were glad of the town's hospitality, but it could not compete with the attraction of the river, because the best was yet to come.

A half day upstream from legendary Thunderhouse Falls, Louis and I decided to ferry across the swiftly moving river and follow a route along the other shore. The others followed in an upstream ferry position, but one of the canoes began dropping closer and closer to the top of the rapid. All we could do was shout, "Paddle harder!" Fortunately they managed to scramble into an eddy. It was a sobering reminder of the river's indifference to poor judgment or lack of skill.

We were lucky. Not so a party travelling ahead of us: two of their group members drowned after going over Thunderhouse Falls.

We heeded signs to pull off the river well above the falls, and to portage through the open pine woods toward the sound of crashing water. At the top of a rise, the anticipation was too much. We dropped our loads and headed out to see what was causing the roar. Thirty metres below us the river pounded with a force that took our breath away.

After exploring the luxurious, moss-covered cliff top, we had lunch on a polished granite shelf by the river, munching in silence while absorbing this stunningly beautiful granite gorge. We were captivated by the awesome power of the river hurtling by us in the glistening sunlight. Knowing we had worked hard to get there made seeing Thunderhouse Falls that much more rewarding — a sweet, good feeling down to our toes.

Below the falls, a solitary stone pillar rises twenty-five metres out of the boiling river. This is "Conjuring House," a place that held religious significance for the native people of this area. Thinking back to the rock

Arrowhead — "Duck Potatoes":
This common river plant has
edible roots that are full of
starch. Indians are said to have
opened muskrat houses to get at
their caches of this wild food.
Canoeists, of course, should opt
for the "pick your own" method.

*"Conjuring House," a solitary
pillar of rock mid-stream below
Thunderhouse Falls, was thought
to have had religious significance
for the local Indians. For
canoeists, this enigmatic butte
provides a handy measuring stick
for comparing water levels.*

paintings on Missinaibi Lake, we wondered what their beliefs and culture had been like before the arrival of the Europeans.

The most challenging white water on the river lies below the falls. We ran five kilometres of continuous rapids that moved briskly between high, rocky hills speckled with a bright green mosaic of moss and lichen. Emerging into a quiet bay, we were exhilarated and relieved to have paddled this section without mishap.

This was a final test, in a way, for our six students. It was now time for them to rely on their own resources and on what they had learned. From here they would be on their own — four days to Moosonee if all went well. Louis and I would follow about half a day behind them, keeping in touch through notes left at preplanned sites.

Alone, Louis and I took time to savour the river valley. Having left the Canadian Shield at Thunderhouse Falls, we paddled across the James Bay lowlands; we began to see white cliffs of sedimentary rock instead of rough granite outcrops. Gradually the river widened and the surrounding landscape became flatter. For the first time we spotted a flock of sandhill cranes. We mused about the progress of the group; but with the current moving us along, sometimes sixty kilometres a day, we had to be careful not to encroach on their earned independence.

We rode the Missinaibi to the place where it joins the Mattagami and becomes the Moose River. Farther down, the Abitibi River makes a dramatic entry, cascading down a series of drops. Near Moosonee, this confluence of rivers spanned nearly three kilometres. Distant sand islands took on a mirage-like quality in moody light. I found myself surprised and intrigued by the changing faces of this portion of the river.

In the late afternoon, twenty-eight days after leaving the shores of Lake Superior, Louis and I rendezvoused with our weary but happy group at Bush Island, near Moosonee. Sitting on the beach, we shared our successes, and what we learned from one another and from the river. After a month of river schooling — working, playing, singing, laughing, disagreeing together — we revelled in a good feeling of closeness and camaraderie. Author Sigurd Olson describes this special canoe-country feeling well:

Left: *Beautiful fruits of a bluebead lily, or yellow clintonia, poke through a fern close to the forest floor. These poisonous berries, named after former New York State Governor DeWitt Clinton, are part of Missinaibi valley flora.*

Below: *Delicate marsh marigolds reach upward to the Missinaibi sun. This plant is found on river banks and along wet sections of portages. Its leaves are sometimes used as pot herbs but require several short boilings with water changes between.*

There would be some things that would never be dimmed by distance or by time, compounded of values that would never be forgotten. The joys and challenges of wilderness, the sense of being part of the country and of an era that was gone. The freedom we had known, silence, timelessness, beauty, companionship, and loyalty and the feeling of fullness and completion that was ours at the end.

Sara Harrison's roots go deep into the wilderness. She has been an instructor and staff trainer at the Voyageur Outward Bound School for six years and an instructor and course director at the Canadian Outward Bound Wilderness School, near Thunder Bay, for four years. Since her 1981 voyage on the Missinaibi, she has led trips on the Misehkow, Albany, Teslin, and Yukon rivers. Other interests include cultural anthropology and dog sledding. Harrison lives in Minneapolis, Minnesota, where she is an interpreter at the Bell Museum of Natural History.

Although river travel and canoes are synonymous for most of us, there are those who explore riparian worlds by other means in other seasons. A canvas wall tent heated by a portable wood stove, lit by candles inside and moonlight outside, looks appealing even at –30°C!

CHAPTER FOUR

WESTERN WILD

North of the prairies, on the Ca-nadian Shield, there are rivers that have drawn travellers for centuries. Rivers such as the Churchill and Fond du Lac were important to the fur trade. Oth-ers, such as the Seal River in northern Manitoba, played a lesser role in the fur trade but attract modern-day voyageurs. The Clearwater rises in north-western Saskatchewan, flows southeast and then west, even-tually entering the Athabasca River at Fort McMurray. Because of its historically important loca-tion at the north end of the noto-rious Methye or La Loche por-tage, between the Hudson Bay and arctic basins, the Clearwater has been nominated as a Cana-dian Heritage River.

Clearwater : Gateway to the North

BY BOB HENDERSON

Canoes and wild rivers are synonymous for most people; but the snowshoe also has a place in the recreational re-exploration of Canada's wild rivers. In the tradition of great winter travellers such as Samuel Hearne, William Butler, and the amazing winter packeteers — Canada's first postmen to deliver mail from the Mackenzie to Montreal — I travelled over the height of land from the Churchill River to the Clearwater River and beyond. This journey took six of us over the epic Methye Portage, an important segment of the early Trans-Canada Highway.

The Methye Portage was the most significant obstacle to the regular fur trade. This twenty-kilometre portage to the Clearwater River is the beginning of the northwest — the "Gateway to the North" William Butler called it in 1870. Paddling the Clearwater was the dream of many a trader and explorer because, by crossing the legendary Methye Portage, novice *mangeurs de lard* — pork eaters — became the more prestigious *hommes du nord*.

Making the crossing was as much my dream as it was for any employee of the North West Company. I had crossed the height of land between the Atlantic and Hudson Bay watersheds many times on canoe routes west of Grand Portage, but only the Clearwater could make the past live again.

Since the Clearwater, I have felt a magical affinity to history and to the land. I now have a sense of cultural fit, as if I was embraced and strengthened by the connections made during that winter on the Clearwater.

Our group was united by a desire for an extended winter trip in a historical context. More practically, as students of the University of Alberta's Exploration Program within the Department of Physical Education, we had field credits to earn. My role as a graduate student was to oversee this winter adventure with an interdisciplinary focus. We selected the La Loche/Clearwater route because of its historic importance.

While there were many individual educational objectives for this enterprise, historical retracing was the common denominator. We knew the river had been a favored winter home for native people due to its abundant wildlife and good hunting. It was a critical link in the fur-

At White Mud Falls on the Clearwater River, author Bob Henderson marvelled at the way ice and water were intertwined in what he saw as 'playful give and take.' This Canadian Heritage River is also a favourite of white-water paddlers in summer.

trade transportation network, and it was used as a corridor to the Arctic by many of the great explorers. During the trip, pathfinders such as George Back, Franklin, and Butler would grow to be more than just historic names. My quest within this vibrant, historical context was described by William C. James: "exploration of the wilderness [is] a voyage into the interior of the self."

We headed north from La Loche town site on a January morning. We felt much as George Back did when he described setting out at the same place 150 years earlier. Back's journal might have been ours:

> *There is something exciting in the first start even upon an ordinary journey. The bustle of preparation — the act of departing, which seems like a decided step taken — the prospect of change, and consequent stretching out of the imagination — have at all times the effect of stirring the blood. . . . Before me were novelty and enterprise; hope, curiosity and the love of adventure were my companions.*

We covered the first sixteen kilometres of the historic Methye Portage in strained, uphill steps. Then, suddenly, against a completely horizontal perspective, we came to the edge of the Clearwater valley. The vertical drop was only 170 metres, but in contrast to the strikingly flat land, it looked much higher. For Franklin, this was one of the "most picturesque" scenes in the northern part of America:

> *We arrived at the summit of a lofty chain of mountains commanding the most picturesque and romantic prospect we had yet seen in this country. Two ranges of high hills ran parallel to each other for several miles until the faint blue haze hides their particular characteristics. The distant prospect is surpassed only in grandeur by the wild scenery that appears immediately below our feet. . . . At one spot, termed the Cockscomb, the passenger stands insulted as it were on a small slip, where a false step might precipitate him into the glen. From this place Mr. Back took an interesting and accurate sketch of the view.*

William Butler was inspired in 1870 not by the beauty of the spot but with the realization that he stood on the edge of immense watersheds and travelways:

> *This long portage . . . is not a bad position from whence to take a bird's eye view of the Great North . . . the only slope is to the North; from here to the frozen sea, 1,000 miles as wild swans fly, is one long, gradual descent.*

Being there, reading this material, searching for the Cockscomb and the site where Back drew his sketch, we were struck by what he called "the genius of the place."

The stillness of winter seemed to originate in the valley. It was as if winter slowly gained momentum as it followed the gradual north slope of the arctic basin. Our pace slowed to about sixteen kilometres per day, and we enjoyed a rest day relaxing in this valley filled with the genius of benign winter.

We winced at Franklin's much more ambitious twenty-five-kilo-metre-per-day pace, but we revelled in the opportunity to have a good look around. The Clearwater was known as a haven for wildlife includ-ing deer, moose, wolf, and bear; but, although I observed winter-kill drama etched in fresh animal tracks, and there were animal signs everywhere, we saw precious little wildlife.

The Methye Portage enters about midway along the length of the Clearwater. In winter, this point in the valley is a meandering white highway, perfect for snowshoeing but not much of a river for white-water enthusiasts. Upstream, though, there are many wild water stretches that draw enthusiastic paddlers in warm weather. And down-stream the river is far from spent.

This rediscovering of history warmed my spirits. I found a rhythm and lyrical meaning in slow-paced snowshoeing. Each day offered long periods of silent travel, favourite.times in which I seemed to melt in the winter landscape. Unloading toboggans, cutting poles, sawing and splitting firewood linked us closely to the land. Of course, we had our down sleeping bags and other twentieth-century trappings, but more than ever before, I had thrown off that other world: our footwear was moosehide moccasins, our clothing wool; our food was traditional, not freeze-dried or prepackaged; and most of our equipment was wood and canvas.

A strange freedom surfaced in this primitive setting, in activity, materials, and desire linked so closely with the land. Traditional style has this reward, but, in its reliance on large amounts of wood for fuel and tent poles, it has a significant impact on the land. Fortunately, winter camps rarely correspond with those used in summer — summer sites are open and exposed, while winter sites must be sheltered, not

In the Clearwater River region the white-tailed deer is at the northern extent of its range. Although up to five million of these animals are shot by hunters or killed by dogs or car collisions each year in North America, multiple litters and early reproductive age allow this animal to be of the most abundant large-game animals.

Left: *Following the tradition of explorers and the winter packeteers, who carried mail between fur-trade posts, an expedition member uses a 6 m tumpline to haul a loaded toboggan.*

Below: *The earliest trade route between eastward- and northward-flowing waters followed the Methye Portage and the Clearwater River. The route was discovered by Peter Pond in 1778 and used for more than a century by fur traders and explorers including Alexander Mackenzie, John Franklin, William Butler and George Simpson.*

right on a waterway — so we were not camping in heavily used locations.

The meandering Clearwater drops thirty metres over Whitemud Falls just beyond the Alberta border. Openings in the ice shrouded in thick mist revealed winter's constant struggle to contain the energy in the falls. Here we took the portage trail, leaving the river for the first time. Uphill hauling in deep snow made us all appreciate the wind-packed snow on the river. With twenty kilometres of intermittent rapids below the falls, we had to read the ice carefully for weak spots.

Downstream, at a limestone gorge, we stopped for a bite. With jaws stiffened by the –20°C temperatures, I read from Franklin's 1820 journal:

> *We afterwards followed the river as far as the Pine Portage, when we passed through a very romantic defile of rocks which presented the appearance of Gothic ruins, and their rude characters were happily contrasted with the softness of the snow, and the darker foliage of the pines which crowned their summits.*

The splintered dolomite pillars before us had to be Franklin's Gothic ruins! Here was a landscape apparently unchanged in more than 150 years; it was as if Franklin had passed through just yesterday. It's sad, but such sites need to be protected to preserve their authenticity. While most of the Saskatchewan portion of the Clearwater is protected by the Canadian Heritage River designation, this Alberta part of the lower river is not.

The Clearwater, like many northern rivers, has not escaped exploitation for economic gain. In the late 1960s, it was decided that the river's hydro power yield was inadequate for development — for the moment — but logging activity downstream was in full swing and would soon shatter our link with the past.

On day 13 our trip was complete. We walked into town, hauling our toboggans along the paved sidewalk to the bus station. But it was more a start than a finish.

As novelist Peter Such wrote:

> *We all need a sense of our past, and how our present and indeed our future grow out, to see ourselves as part of that continuing tradition as it keeps evolving and not separate from it.*

Waxing runners using a candle and a heated axehead stops icing and makes heavy loads easier to haul.

To this Grey Owl can add:

> *Each succeeding generation takes on the works by those who pass along leaving behind them a tradition and a standard of achievement, that must be lived up to by those who would claim a membership in the Brotherhood of the Keepers of the Trail.*

This winter trek on the Clearwater showed me that there really is a "Brotherhood of the Keepers of the Trail"; indeed, we all need a sense of the past to evolve wisely as culture and wilderness clash on so many fronts. Perhaps it is as Keepers of the Trail we can build a culture better adapted to our needs in nature and the needs of such wild places. The Clearwater was my beginning. For the first time I saw the land and its heritage not from the outside looking in but as part of the inside.

Bob Henderson canoed his way through Lakefield College School and McMaster University before joining the University of Alberta Master's program which took him down the Clearwater in the winter of 1980. From 1973 to 1980, he was a summer canoe-tripping guide at Camp Ahmek in Ontario's Algonquin Provincial Park. Since then he has rediscovered historical routes from Tasmania to Baffin Island. Henderson lives in Dundas, Ontario, where he is a Lecturer in Outdoor Education at McMaster University.

Lynx: Studies have shown that this resident of the Clearwater valley is actually more efficient at hunting rabbits and hares in winter than in any other season. Wide furry paws act as snowshoes; the lynx's long legs move with ease through deep snow and its muted colours blend into a winter forest's gloom. What looks like a bushy tail in this photograph is actually the well-insulated inside of an outstretched back leg.

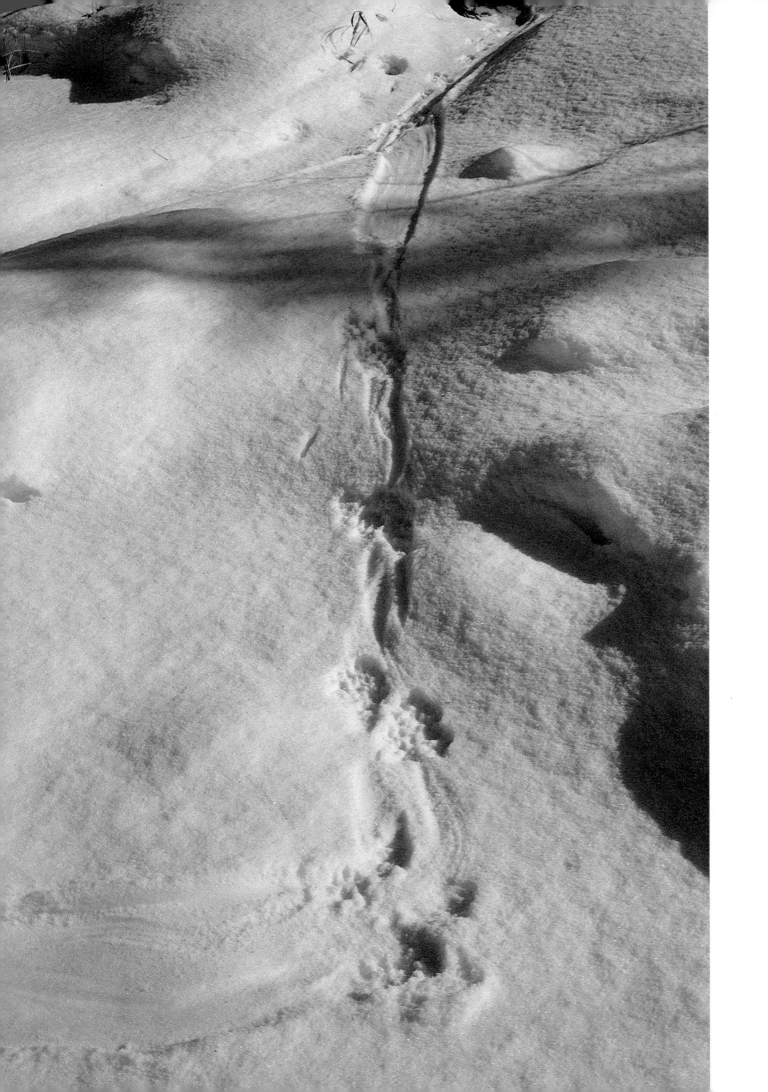

Opposite: *Playful in winter, too, the river otter saves time and energy by folding its front legs back and sliding along on the snow. Even going up hill, this animal manages to get in a few slips between steps.*

Below: *A Swainson's hawk crouches over winter kill.*

Kazan Falls.

CHAPTER FIVE

BARREN LAND WILD

Beyond the limit of Canada's forests, great northern rivers sweep through austere tundra lands east to Hudson Bay and north to the Arctic Ocean. The Thelon, Dubawnt, Kazan, and Back rivers are known for their exploration history and for abundant wildlife. These waterways are remote and unforgiving — the ultimate wilderness-canoe challenges.

Kazan : River of the Living Barrens

BY DAVID F. PELLY

D escending the Kazan River in the Northwest Territories you sense the ethereal presence of past inhabitants. There are no people on the river banks; this is real wilderness. But the route is marked with piles of stones left by the people who travelled this river in a time now lost but not distant. *Inuksuit*, or *inukshuks* meaning "likenesses of men," stand erect against the horizon and guide travellers along the shores of expansive arctic lakes to where water rejoins the swiftly flowing rivers. For today's paddler, the *inuksuit* are the only remaining likeness of the people who once lived along this great river.

On the eighth day of a fifty-one-day, 1000-kilometre trip down the Kazan in 1982, I went for a walk — as is my habit. Climbing a small rise inland from our campsite, I encountered an unnatural pile of rocks overgrown with scrub birch and willow. As I looked more closely, my eyes met the hollow stare of a skull within the rock-pile. In the time-honoured way of his people, this hunter had been laid to rest on a hilltop, probably overlooking his hunting ground, his body simply covered with a mound of rocks. Decades later, all that remained after the foxes took their fill was this stately stare. This was my introduction to the people who built the *inuksuit* of the Kazan.

There are other magnificent rivers in the Barren Lands, to be sure. Together they represent nearly 5000 kilometres of wilderness paddling. On the Thelon you are virtually assured of seeing musk-ox, an unforgettable thrill for any wildlife buff. The Back has been described as the wildest of Canada's wild rivers; certainly it is one of the remotest and least travelled. All these rivers conjure images of the extraordinary feats of early European explorers. But for me, the Kazan stands out because here I felt like a visitor to the camps, the hunting grounds, the trails, the lookouts, and the graves of the inland Inuit.

Probably during the eighteenth century, these people abandoned the sea coasts and moved onto the Barrens. They developed a dependence on caribou for their food, clothing, shelter, transportation, and tools. A caribou shoulder, for example, would first be cleaned of its meat; then the blade-like bone would be used to scrape skins. These skins would then be dried and sewn together with sinew to make a summer tent. During the last thirty years, most inland Inuit abandoned the skin tents

Inuksuit *or "stone man" was used by the Inuit for navigation over land and for herding caribou toward hidden hunters. Their age and authenticity can be determined by the maturity and composition of the lichen community growing on the* component rocks. *It is rumoured that in recent times, a bushwacked northern pilot took sadistic pleasure in erecting* inuksuit *when he landed on tundra lakes, muttering, "That'll fix those damn archaeologists!"*

and moved to settlements, drawn by trading posts and missions; but that many of these people used to live in the Kazan valley suggests that the area has long supported an abundance of caribou.

Today the Kaminuriak caribou herd, which takes it name from the highland calving grounds near Kaminuriak Lake east of the lower Kazan, is thought to number 300,000. From our campsite atop a high bank on day 37, we watched a stream of caribou move across a low plain on the other side of the river. Through binoculars we could count 100 or more at any time, grazing as they flowed over the tundra. During dinner and mug-up before bed, we saw at least 1,000 caribou move by. The migration continued most of the night. In the days that followed, we often saw caribou that covered the rolling prairie just beyond the river bank.

As raw and removed from southern technology as our paddle on the Kazan seemed, with herds of caribou and visions of Inuit hunters filling our days, we couldn't deny the dramatic changes this wilderness has seen during the twentieth century. We often reflected on our earliest predecessors' experiences. When the Tyrrell brothers paddled their Peterborough canoes down the Kazan in 1894, in the service of the Geological Survey of Canada, they were not all that different in their mode of travel. But what a different world they saw.

Caribou were plentiful along most of the river and formed an important part of the explorers' diet. J.B. Tyrrell's hand-written journal (now in the University of Toronto's rare book collection) makes frequent reference to their success at the hunt, and describes such places as Palenah, just upstream from Yathkyed Lake, "where the river is narrow and deep with a fair current, a famous place for the Eskimo to spear deer [caribou] in the water." Tyrrell watched a hunter named Ahyout manoeuvre his kayak among the caribou herd as they crossed the river. Carefully choosing his prey, Ahyout plunged his spear between the caribou's ribs, piercing its lung, leaving it just enough life to make the shore, while the hunter continued his work. At every camp he passed, Tyrrell saw meat drying on the rocks or cached for the winter. In all, he visited thirty-nine tents housing many of the 500 people who lived by the Kazan.

In 1982 we saw the lichen-covered stones of fifty-two abandoned tent rings. We saw sun-bleached caribou bones scattered on the ground at old campsites. We stood over the graves of fourteen former dwellers of the Barren Lands; but it is the first, that lonely skull beneath a pile of

Left: *An Inuit grave site halfway along the Kazan River on the north shore of Angikuni Lake. Wooden parts of a sled and kayak, perhaps those of the deceased, lie amongst the burial rocks.*

Below left: *Modern-day camper fries a breakfast over a fire of heat-rich tundra twigs.*

Below: *Yesterday's camp: An old chest of possessions and trading goods left beside an overgrown Inuit grave site on the Kazan River.*

rocks, that remains fixed in my mind. Yet we met not another living soul, save our fellow canoeists; and our caribou sightings — spectacular as we thought them — were restricted to a few fortunate days when we intersected the movement of the main body of the Kaminuriak population. The last great wilderness of North America *has* changed.

The treeless land through which the Kazan flows is, however, still an awe-inspiring wilderness. For me, no sensation can match that of standing atop an esker coursing its way across the tundra, and absorbing the surrounding world. Inevitably there are birds — spirited longspurs chirping at my feet, magnificent raptors screaming overhead — 100 or more species annually migrate to nesting grounds on the Barren Lands.

On a warm day the sun beats on the rich vegetation, which grows within only inches of the surface; a wonderfully fresh and penetrating fragrance rises to your nostrils. It is that unique smell that, more than any other single factor, typifies summer on the Barrens for me. When the sun shines nearly around the clock, every day brings new flowers to the tundra. Mountain avens — the flower of the Northwest Territories — are among the first to bloom, in June; dwarf fireweed, lasting into August, is one of the last. The season is short but dramatic. Standing up on the esker, one looks out over thousands of square kilometres of wilderness which, despite its popular name and the utter absence of trees, is anything but barren of life.

The system that all this life comprises is one of the most fragile on earth. The mean temperature is low; the annual precipitation rarely exceeds twenty-five centimetres. The soil is somewhat sterile, being largely deprived of the advantages of organic decay. Strong arctic winds dry the air and bombard the plants' exposed surfaces with sand and snow. Yet this fragile system exhibits a powerful beauty, which is never more profoundly felt than by standing on the land, by walking across it.

Hiking is an important part of the Barren Lands canoeing experience. To paddle down any of these mighty arctic rivers and not take time to hike up onto the tundra is to miss one of the unique features of such a trip. Being on the land is what brings you close to the life of the Barrens.

One afternoon our Kazan party hiked to a hilltop from which we enjoyed a view out over Yathkyed Lake, the largest open-water crossing on the river. It was July 27, when the lake can still be frozen. Indeed, the Inuit name for the lake is Hikulijuaq, meaning "the great ice-filled one." We were eager to climb to the summit because it would provide us with

A tundra swan (formerly called whistling swan) takes off from its Kazan River nesting site. Smaller than its more common relative the trumpeter swan, this bird breeds across the Canadian Arctic.

our first glimpse of the lake, which had been on our minds as a barrier, both physical and psychological, for some days.

We saw no ice. Our way was clear! We stood pondering the expanse of water stretching beyond the horizon, and we were brought closer by our experience. In time, we spread out across our hilltop, each seeking some moments of independent solitude — rare and treasured moments away from the group's interdependence, so intensely exaggerated by the isolation of the Barrens.

Back together we shared new discoveries — a couple of new species of flowers, moss campion and alpine azalea. We discussed building a cairn or leaving a message under a rock, but decided to leave the landscape unmarred. On the way back down to the canoes, we collected some scraps of wood to use in a baking fire that evening.

Canoeing the Barren Lands tends to be filled with such special moments — some pleasant, some profoundly unpleasant. Sitting in the tent, the walls straining in like a topgallant on a square-rigger running before the wind, a storm howling, pellets of icy rain beating relentlessly against the taut nylon shield between me and the outside, I endure the discomfort by forcing myself to remember the pleasures of the Barrens. Betting that the moorings of my shelter will hold, I muse thankfully on the extra five minutes I devoted to anchoring the tent before the storm began. It will end, in time, perhaps as suddenly as it arose. That is the nature of the Barren Lands: changeable, unpredictable, untamed, utterly wild.

One day all eight of us huddled together under a pair of upturned canoes as hailstones pelted our refuge. A few days later we ran barefoot on a trackless beach in heat that made even the frigid arctic waters tempting.

It is a world into which one must not venture without adequate preparation — not just the physical readiness needed for every canoe trip. This wilderness demands a certain attitude, an awareness that nature is going to be supreme. One must bend to its whims; one must approach the Barrens as a visitor, not a conqueror. Indeed, travel on the Barrens, summer or winter, is a humbling experience, as one realizes one's impotence before nature. Nowhere, in my experience, is life so dictated by the elements.

On the exposed waters of an arctic lake a sudden wind can easily

Right: *Forest dwellers often see the tundra as a blank, as the land is treeless and flat. On closer inspection, one sees diverse flora thriving in a sheltered micro-climate on top of the permafrost. Here, cloudberries and labrador tea poke through a mat of coloured mosses.*

Below: *First cousin to the great fighting trout and the magnificent salmon, the arctic char is known for the change in coloration that occurs as it approaches spawning condition. At this time, body colour deepens from pinky silver to brilliant orange. The leading edges of lower fins turn white and males develop a salmon-like protruding hook on the lower jaw. This fish is ready for spawning . . . and eating.*

*A lone gull watches over a
typical ledge on the Kazan River.*

whip up waves that make paddling both uncomfortable and dangerous; it might blow for days. Patience is the only remedy, a lesson well taken from the Inuit dwellers of the Barrens, who survived in part through the application of great patience. Today's optimistic Barren Lands traveller looks upon such windbound occasions as ideal times to go hiking, while the bugs have taken shelter.

In this regard the Kazan is not unlike the Back or the Thelon. There are, however, ways in which the Kazan differs from its sister rivers of the arctic prairie. Its character is the most varied of any arctic river I have seen. Every day brings new landforms, from canyons to gently rolling hills to marshy lowlands where walking is hopping from hummock to hillock. The river itself changes from wild white water to lazy current, and provides comfortably spaced breaks from confined river travel, traversing occasional lakes, large and small.

In a few stretches, the river sweeps along at such a speed that paddling becomes superfluous. There are a few mighty cataracts and the climatic Kazan Falls, which can be admired only from the shore, and many rapids that can be handled by the skilled canoeist. Conditions change dramatically from year to year, depending on snowfall during the preceding winter and the date of the spring break-up (usually mid-June in the swiftly flowing sections). This uncertainty demands that the wilderness traveller assess each rapid as it is encountered. The price of taking a chance, and losing, is simply too high in the isolation of the Barren Lands rivers.

Historically the wild rivers of Canada were the threads that tied together a nation. Today they provide the arteries by which we can penetrate the wilderness, in a process which is arguably quintessentially Canadian. The wild rivers are more than a valuable resource to Canada, more than an important element of our heritage; they are part of our life.

The Kazan, more than any river to the south, more than other rivers of the north paddled before and since, was the river that took me farthest away from my usual community, brought me closest to the land. On that land, removed from my own society, I was exposed to the heritage of one group of original Canadians. I implore all paddlers who follow the route to show the greatest respect for the archeological remains that lie beside the Kazan, for only in this way can we preserve a unique element of the Canadian heritage.

At the river's end in the hamlet of Baker Lake, I met the proud

Labrador tea, sometimes called Hudson's Bay tea in northern Canada, is a hardy plant easily recognized by the woolly brown undersurfaces of its leaves.

descendants of the Kazan people, in their present-day society. Nothing could have been a more fitting conclusion, nor a more apt process. First I experienced their land; then I saw the physical evidence of their history. Then I met the people. That is how it should be.

In the traditions of his explorer ancestors, Lieutenant-Commander David F. Pelly retired from the Navy after ten years of active service and turned his attention to major summer expeditions on the Back, Kazan, and Thelon rivers, and winter sled trips with his Inuit friends. Books resulting from these northern experiences include Expedition: An Arctic Journey Through History on George Back's River *(1981) and* Qikaaluktut: Images of Inuit Life *(1986, with R.A. Tulurialik). Pelly, a Fellow of the Royal Geographical Society, is a free-lance writer, alternating between Baker Lake, Northwest Territories, and his home in Castleton, Ontario.*

Arctic reflections: Author Mason's companions set out across calm and open headwaters of the Hood River. Favourable winds have kept pack ice pinned against the opposite shore, leaving a wide lead for making headway toward the river.

ARCTIC WILD

Above the Arctic Circle in the central Northwest Territories is the region where Sir John Franklin and his men made their epic explorations in the early 1800s. Franklin left Fort Enterprise, near Great Slave Lake, and travelled north via the Coppermine River. Paddling bark canoes, they mapped the coast of the Arctic Ocean east of the Coppermine and eventually struggled south again up a river named for Franklin's steadfast midshipman, Robert Hood. Modern-day canoeists usually follow Franklin down the Coppermine River; a smaller number have sought kinship with Franklin in the valleys of the Hood, Burnside, and Mara rivers. These are remote rivers with ice-cold wild water and compelling historical intrigue.

Hood: In Franklin's Wake

BY BILL MASON

I awoke to the sound of steadily pounding arctic rain, which, I sensed, would continue for days. It's strange how you can tell. My five companions — Wally Schaber, Bruce Cockburn, Gilles Lebreque, Alan Whatmough, and Gilles Couet — were still asleep, or pretending to be. I rolled over in the luxurious warmth of my bag and revelled in the feeling of remoteness and unlimited distance that brought us here.

For the first time since our Hood River trip began, we didn't have to break camp. We had two days in our schedule to enjoy the spectacular scenery around Wilberforce Falls, rain or no. The day before we had all agreed, despite overcast light, that this fifty-metre falls and four-kilometre canyon was the most spectacular sight we had ever seen, better even than Virginia Falls on the Nahanni River.

Until the summer of 1983, my favourite canoe trip was a toss-up between two Lake Superior rivers: the Pukaskwa and the Dog River with spectacular Denison Falls. I still favor those trips for pure enjoyment, but the Hood pumped adrenalin through my veins at record rates.

The Hood flows from west to east for several hundred kilometres through the central Northwest Territories, parallelling the arctic coastline about 160 kilometres inland from the Arctic Ocean. Just before Bathurst Inlet, the river does a right-angle turn and crashes north over Wilberforce Falls into Arctic Sound.

We were concerned that even in July the lakes would still be locked in ice. We dreaded the possibility of being ice-bound; we badly wanted to spend our only two days to spare at Wilberforce Falls. We had heard stories of people being stuck for weeks and having to haul laden canoes over ice floes.

We were very fortunate. Our Yellowknife-based pilot was able to land in the headwaters of the river; while we were on these lakes, a steady northwest wind kept chunks of ice pinned against the south shore, leaving a narrow lead along the north shore. Occasionally we had to make a short haul over ice when the lead closed, but compared to the trip reports we'd read, our entry to the Hood was smooth.

There are two basic kinds of terrain through which the river flows. There is difficult walking terrain — grassy hummocks sitting in icy

A seldom-seen treasure of the Hood River is a second channel at Wilberforce Falls that runs only when water is high. In the red quartzite rock, a lucky traveller can find small deposits of semi-precious amethyst.

water, not quite strong enough to support a person's weight. Hummocks make for cold, wet feet and sore ankles. The other terrain is a delight to walk on — meandering ridges of sand and gravel, called eskers, that snake for great distances over the treeless landscape. These mark the location of rivers that flowed beneath the last great ice sheets.

The wet terrain was home to healthy populations of mosquitoes. When the weather was cold, warm clothing protected us, but still our faces, hands, and necks were exposed. Strong winds gave relief from the bugs, but occasionally they were intolerable. Most times, though, the scenery, the river, the rapids, the caribou, the musk-ox, the food, and the fun made the mosquitoes easier to take.

My greatest delight was to finish supper early and set out on long hikes. From most eskers I could see several days' journey in all directions. Sometimes I could almost see Sir John Franklin and his men trekking toward the south in August 1821, carrying their one battered canoe, trying to follow the eskers back to Fort Enterprise after an epic summer of discovery. What might it have been that drove them to leave their homes in England to explore this barren, hostile, and cruel landscape? I also thought of how these explorers chose not to adopt the ways of the native people, who made this forbidding land home by following the migrating herds of caribou.

I thought of Franklin's desperate plight. They were out of food and winter had come early; for more than half of them it was a death march. Midshipman Hood fell behind. When one of the guides showed up with fresh meat, Franklin became suspicious: it was Hood. The guide had shot him; and he, in turn, had to be executed. Just the thought of these events sent shivers up my spine.

The region is described as "barren," yet we saw more wildlife in one trip than I've seen in a lifetime of southern canoeing. The diversity of living creatures may be low, but the numbers are staggering. It's difficult to describe the thrill of paddling by thousands of caribou. The caribou were travelling along the north shore of the Hood toward the west. We were travelling east and it took two days to paddle by the herd. We were amazed that such terrain could support these vast herds. The secret of their success is migration, an amazing mechanism that prevents them from overbrowsing.

Encountering musk-ox was another highlight of the trip. We saw many individuals as well as groups of two, three, and four. The largest groups were nine and ten and usually had calves among them.

Although wolves north of the tree line are informally called "tundra wolves," to differentiate them from the timber wolf that lives below the tree line and the arctic wolf that lives on the arctic islands, all these dog-like carnivores belong to the same genus and species, Canis lupus. For tundra wolves the most important prey animal is caribou.

Barren-ground caribou step lightly away from approaching canoeists. Like all four sub-species of caribou that live in the Northwest Territories, both male and female barren-ground caribou have antlers that are shed and re-grown every year. These animals are members of the Bathurst Herd (approximately 180,000 strong) that winters below the tree line north of Great Slave Lake and calves, after a long annual migration, on the east side of Bathurst Inlet.

Left: *With no trees in the arctic, birds must nest on the ground, which requires good camouflage colouring. These semi-palmated plover eggs blend in nicely. They are also purposely oriented with small ends toward the centre of the nest. Some scientists think that this four-egg pattern makes the clutch easier for the adults to incubate; others postulate that the pattern is a heat-saving adaptation that reduces airflow over the eggs when the nest is unattended.*

Below: *From high land above this campsite on the Hood, it is possible to see several days' journey in all directions.*

Left: *River beauty — a showy far-northern relative of fireweed that grows on gravelly river banks across the arctic.*

Below: *A scenic and historic river named by explorer Sir John Franklin after his Midshipman Robert Hood. Almost dead from a diet of shoe leather and lichen, Hood was shot and killed on October 20, 1821 near this location by his tentmate Michel Terohaute, an Iroquois Indian.*

The brink of Wilberforce Falls: two falls totalling more than 65 m are thought to be the highest falls in the world north of the Arctic Circle. Here, there are no barriers to stop curious onlookers from falling over the edge.

We had it on authority that musk-ox rarely charge; they are much more likely to run away. On one occasion we saw two musk-ox in a clump of willows. Alan, Bruce, Gilles, and I went up onto a ridge where they could see us. Wally and Gilles Couet sneaked through the metre-high willows to get a picture of them. The musk-ox turned to look in the direction of their approach. Wally and Gilles were not going unnoticed, but there was no way to tell them! With cameras ready, Wally and Gilles peeked around from behind the willows. There, staring right back at them barely ten metres away, were two confused musk-ox! All of a sudden they butted their heads together and turned to look back at Wally and Gilles. Wally made a swath through the willows back to the canoes; Gilles widened it. We never did convince Wally and Gilles that head butting is anything but a preliminary act to all-out charge.

Although we never saw a wolf, we saw many wolf scats and footprints. For me, the presence of wolves is a sign that all is well and in a natural state. We were also privileged to catch a glimpse of a peregrine falcon. Whenever I see one I am touched with sadness that they are so rare.

The rapids were runnable, Class I to Class III. There were a few that we chose to line because of the frigid water and air temperatures. Moreover, losing a canoe or having an injury would turn an enjoyable trip into a nightmare. It was with great reluctance and disappointment that we lined our first rapid, but our disappointment was short-lived; almost everything else that wasn't classified as a falls proved to be runnable.

We were approaching a set described in our trip notes as "absolutely unrunnable." We pulled over to the left shore in preparation for a landing. But no, not yet! Ahead was a huge boulder jutting out into the current. You could see calm water just beyond the rock. The two Gilles drifted their canoe right by the rock and back-paddled into the eddy. It wasn't that difficult but there was no room for error; the eddy was just above the brink of a wild rapid.

We set up for the back ferry and followed suit. We drifted by the rock and a couple of hefty backstrokes put us in the eddy. I looked back for Alan and Bruce and was horrified to see that the current had grabbed their canoe and swung it right out into centre stream. They had no choice but to attempt a run!

Wally, the two Gilles, and I wouldn't have bet a nickel on their chances of getting through upright or in one piece, even with their spray

Right: *Mason's compadres settle in for a feed of fresh lake trout.*

Below: *Long portages across tundra inspire novel transportation solutions. These portagers are using what is affectionately known as the "Jimmy Hoffa Method."*

cover. We would have to get there quickly to rescue them from the ice-cold water. Yet we couldn't move; we were horror-struck. They plummeted down into the maelstrom of plunging waves and almost disappeared. Slowly the canoe surfaced with water pouring off the decks like a submarine. They were still upright! They disappeared and reappeared once more — still upright. They emerged at the bottom still floating, but just. We were ecstatic, laughing and shouting as we leaped into our canoes for a sneak run tight to the shore, anxious to get to them before they sank.

They had shot something as extreme as anything I've ever seen; they hit it dead centre where the rocks were all buried. They had kept their balance and powered through — no fancy manoeuvres — but we still believed they might sink before reaching shore. As we rounded the bend, there was Alan reclining on a pack on shore smoking his pipe. Bruce was wringing out some clothes. Alan said with utter disdain, "I see you took the easy route." We all cracked up! The two least-experienced canoeists had run a rapid that looked more like a falls.

There was one other stretch of rapids that we debated about running, a long gorge with several small waterfalls. In bright sunshine the rapids looked turbulent but inviting. We decided to portage all the gear to the end and run the rapids empty after lunch. As we ate a leisurely lunch on a high knoll overlooking the gorge, the sunlight gave way to grey cloud. My enthusiasm for running the turbulent rapid waned with the dropping temperature. I was relieved when Wally asked, "How badly do you want to run that?" I looked up at the grey sky and said, "Not very." We decided to portage, but how we hated to waste a good run.

When we looked back up the rapid there was Gilles Lebreque taking one last look. He decided to try it solo. We grabbed our cameras and recorded Gilles making every move exactly as planned. I looked again at the cold bleak sky and decided that I wasn't heartbroken that we hadn't tried. I only wished Gilles hadn't made it look so easy.

As enthusiastic as we were about running rapids, we were never disappointed when the sound of distant white water turned out to be a thundering waterfall. I can sit for days watching them and I love to clamber over rocks and view, photograph, and sketch them from every conceivable angle. Most of the waterfalls on the Hood were preceded or followed by a gorge. Because of the absence of trees it was very easy to view them from any angle, but it wasn't until one of us stood beside the falls that we got any sense of scale.

Prior to Mason's Hood River trip, Wilberforce Canyon had never been paddled. Somehow (the crew won't say) they got into a large eddy below the falls. This picture documents the start of a first attempt at shooting the canyon.

Apart from the scenery, it was the light that set the mood. The sun hardly dipped below the horizon so we enjoyed more than four hours of warm twilight glow. The cold austere landscape took on the warm colour of the sky. Bleak rock faces shone like gold. Often the wind dropped at night to a gentle whisper. It was a time of magic.

The fact that you can see for miles and miles in all directions makes the land feel limitless, yet it is so fragile. It could never sustain or absorb great numbers of people. It has always amazed me that the native people, though here for thousands of years, somehow kept their numbers more or less constant in relation to their source of food. Yet our well-being depends on increased growth in the economy and population. The end result can only be overcrowding and depletion of resources, all at the expense of the environment and the other creatures that share the earth with us.

On the Hood, we were the only human beings within hundreds of kilometres, yet we were deeply aware of the impact that just six of us had on the land. Camped at Wilberforce Falls before our final run to the sea, it was an effort to find enough wood just to heat a pail of soup or a pot of tea. We also cooked with a gas stove, but we really enjoyed the small fire. Yet we all realized how quickly the shore could be denuded of firewood.

The sheer size of the land and its remoteness from our world have kept it relatively unchanged; but what was once a journey of one or two years just to get here from the south can now be accomplished in two days from Ottawa. Now it's only the cost of getting here that protects the land from overuse. With the high cost, ice-coated lakes, mosquitoes, and black-flies, I doubt that the land will ever be overrun with sight-seers. Still, it is difficult to look on this land and its varied life and not care about what happens to it.

Bill Mason is a man of many talents who captured North American hearts with films and books that share his love for the canoe and sensitivity to the wilderness. As a filmmaker, he is best known for his Path of the Paddle *series. He has won fifty-eight national and international awards, including two British Academy Awards and two Oscar nominations. After the release of his last film,* Waterwalker, *Mason retired from the National Film Board and turned his full attention to writing and painting. Mason's home and studio are near Old Chelsea, Quebec, north of Ottawa.*

*A brilliant sunset turns the
waters of the Bonnet Plume
burnt orange behind the
silhouette of canoe and paddle.*

CHAPTER SEVEN

MOUNTAIN WILD

There are many wild rivers in the Yukon that rise high in the Rockies. Some make their way to the Pacific as tributaries of the Yukon River, others to the Beaufort Sea as tributaries of the Mackenzie. But on the north slope of the continent are rivers such as the Blackstone, Ogilvie, Wind, Snake, and Bonnet Plume, which flow north to the Peel.

Bonnet Plume:
Homeland of the Loucheux

BY C.E.S. FRANKS

Unlike more famous northern rivers, the Bonnet Plume is associated with no history of exploration or legends of great and tragic deeds. It is one of the hundreds of small rivers that flow through the Canadian wilderness, hardly touched by man. It is also one of the most beautiful. From its source high in the mountains of the Continental Divide, it flows due north through the Yukon until it meets the Peel. The first 240 kilometres from the put-in at Bonnet Plume Lake are in a narrow valley between mountains. Then the relief becomes lower, the valley wider. The river drops more than three metres per kilometre, making it fast and, potentially, very dangerous.

It took two trips for an Otter to carry six of us, our gear, and three canoes from Mayo in the Yukon to Bonnet Plume Lake. I arrived on the second trip, with Shawn Hodgins and Saundra Raymond, after nine in the evening. The mountains surrounding the lake were speckled with light and shadow, set off by towering cumulus clouds. Peter Milliken and Bob and Helene Edwards had gone in on the first flight. Tents were set up near an outfitter's camp; grayling and lake trout fillets were frying for dinner.

We would spend two days beside the lake hiking, fishing, and taking in the scenery before starting down the river on our 520-kilometre journey to Fort McPherson, near the Peel/Mackenzie confluence. While camped, we met two other wilderness travellers, who had flown in a few days earlier. They were to catch up with the other two of their crew in a day or so. As it turned out, our pace on the river was about the same, and we met each other frequently at camps, on rapids, or on the water. They were good company and didn't make the river crowded.

Another meeting came on our second day at the campsite. Shawn and I were fishing for grayling in the creek that flows from the lake to the Bonnet Plume River. The fishing was almost too good. I was catching a feisty little grayling with nearly every fly cast. This soon gave me more than we needed and was becoming boring. I heard some noise, and looked up to see a dog (at first I thought it was a wolf) and three men on horseback. They were guides, bringing in horses and supplies to the outfitters' camp for the hunting season.

The Bonnet Plume rises high in the Mackenzie Mountains of the continental divide, dropping 91 m in 530 km.

Overleaf: *Campfire pans on the Bonnet Plume are often filled with fillets of arctic grayling, a small yet feisty fish. The milky colour of the water in this photograph is due to silt from mountain glaciers.*

*In its first 100 km, the Bonnet
Plume crashes through four
canyons. Choosing not to shoot
canyon rapids can lead to
another set of little problems.*

They had ridden in from Macmillan Pass, more than 150 kilometres
to the south, near the headwaters of the Nahanni. It had taken them
twelve days to make the trip. The outfitter they work for has rights to
11 200 square kilometres of mountain country, and during the eight-
week season they host up to four trophy hunters at a time, who fly in on
two-week hunts for moose, caribou, bear, or Dall's sheep. The hunters
pay up to $10,000 each; to the guides, who go back south to Alberta and
California after the season ends, the two-month stay in the Yukon is a
paid vacation.

The guides soon had a spotting scope out, and in short order we were
all watching a sow grizzly and her cub hunting for ground squirrels on a
mountainside several miles away. These bears hibernate for eight
months of the year, the guides told us.

Next morning we had a relaxed cup of coffee with the guides, said our
goodbyes, and began down the river. We were a little apprehensive
because we'd heard reports of a challenging run through a huge mud
and rock slide that filled the valley. Centuries ago, the river had carved a
three-kilometre piece off the face of the mountains. (The previous year,
one crew had taken two days to get through and had suffered a very
dangerous capsize.) The photos we'd seen didn't make the river look as
difficult as that, but we were still a little nervous. I think even the best
canoeists are mildly nervous at the beginning of a long trip on a strange
river. You never know what lies ahead. And tales of the horrors and
terrors others have experienced don't reduce the nervousness.

We came to the gorge after an hour of paddling. The day was sunny
and warm. As we entered it we kept our ears open for the deeper sound
of impassable rapids or waterfalls, but we didn't hear it. We hugged the
inner shore as the river meandered around innumerable bends, and we
scouted one piece from a ledge. An hour later we were at the end. No
problems. Elated. Ran everything else until we camped beside a small
creek thirty kilometres from where we'd begun. Pizza for dinner and
rum toddies for comfort and cheer.

The next two days followed the same pattern. Spectacular scenery,
many sets of Class II and III rapids, a few short portages, a meeting with
our fellow travellers.

On the fourth day we reached the canyon that was supposed to
require a 1.5-kilometre portage. We had seen slides of a friend's trip on
the Bonnet Plume, replete with dumps in cold, formidable-looking
water, anxiety about making the schedule, bad weather, and twenty-

Left: *On the edge of the tree line, the Bonnet Plume provides excellent opportunities for hiking.*

Below: *Members of Franks' expedition shoot a set of rapids on the Bonnet Plume.*

hour days to make up lost time. Some of us had also seen a TV film of a cold, miserable-looking crew travelling down the same river and obviously having great difficulty handling the rapids.

Sometimes we wondered whether we were on the right river. Here we were at a "compulsory" portage around one of the most difficult rapids. We looked it over. The river was in a deep gorge, but we scrambled along the bank and found that, after a first short piece of dangerous, rock-filled rapids, there was an exciting Class III rapid, a short carry, and then what looked like an easy run out to the end. Shawn, the youngest of us at twenty-three but also the best white-water canoeist, had pointed out that if we crossed to the far side at the top we had only to lift our canoes over a small drop; then we could run the rapids down to the carry around the falls.

Two of our canoes did this. The third elected to portage. We found it wasn't all that simple, requiring precise manoeuvring in the heavy water and a careful eddy turn and landing above the falls. The party we were sharing the river with also ran. One of them hit a rock and got unpleasantly full of water; but they too managed to pull out.

We sat in the bright sunlight and had lunch, the sparkle of the mist from the falls behind us, their quiet roar a constant background sound. A grayling, curious about the intrusion, came up to the surface of the milky water and sampled some crumbs. We examined the Mad River ABS canoe that had banged the rock and found a tear in the tough outer vinyl. Nothing serious, but more damage than expected.

This was the end of the difficult water. All we had to do from now on was stay on the river: the current would get us to the end even if we hardly lifted a paddle. We now had a week of comfortable, relaxed canoeing to get to Fort McPherson. The river was ours to enjoy.

On every canoe trip there is a time when you begin to come to terms with a river. Each river has its own character. Some are unfriendly and have long, hard portages and sparse, stunted fish; others are idyllic and easy. The Bonnet Plume, we had learned, was not a difficult river, though it did require careful judgment and decisive manoeuvring. It was running at a good speed and would take us where we wanted with little effort. The snow-topped mountains, a wooded river valley, the full bloom of the wildflowers of arctic summer, and plentiful fish and wildlife were spectacular. The weather, which is much more fickle in these mountains of the Yukon than on the Barren Lands to the east of

the Mackenzie River, had been mostly good. We and the river were on good terms, and there appeared to be no reason for us not to remain so.

As we neared the end of yet another canyon, a huge bald eagle flew up from a gravel bar. A good omen. During the following days there was some rain, but most of the time it was sunny with enough wind to keep the bugs down. I used bug repellent only three times during the trip. One day after lunch we saw seven white Dall's sheep winding their way around the mountainside 300 metres above us. Another day a woodland caribou with a magnificent set of antlers came to inspect our campsite. Once, a wolf kept watch on us for a while, and soon afterward a moose ambled away through the bush at a pace a man couldn't match.

We were beginning to leave the cares of the south behind us. For the first days we'd slept ten to twelve hours. Now we were down to eight. The river broadened, and the mountains grew lower and more distant. As we approached the Peel River, nine days after landing at Bonnet Plume Lake, the river divided into many channels in a sixteen-kilometre-long delta of rocks and gravel. The river here was very fast. I measured its speed one morning at ten kph as it streamed past the campsite. It stayed fast as it rushed down the delta, zigzagging from side to side like a skier traversing to slow a steep descent.

Normally a canoeist is at the lowest point of a valley. If you can't see what's ahead, you feel uneasy. If you see a horizon line across the river you feel more than uneasy; you stop and look. On these last kilometres of the Bonnet Plume we could see the river dropping as it raced ahead of us. But we could also see a horizon line to the side, where the delta dropped faster than the river. This isn't normal. I kept expecting the river to fall off; but it never did, and soon we reached the Peel.

It was browner than the Bonnet Plume, and at times we could hear a sound like light rain on a tent; it was silt hitting the bottom of the canoe. Not all wilderness rivers are clear, and I had to remind myself that one should not make the mistake of assuming nature never erodes or pollutes. The Peel soon entered a gorge with 150-metre cliffs lining a winding channel. A little care was needed to avoid the heavy standing waves, but we spent more time marvelling at the cliffs than worrying about the rapids.

As we rounded that last bend we were hit full in the face by a fierce headwind; so, even though it was only 3:00 P.M., we retreated behind the shelter of the last point of the canyon cliffs and camped. The site

Overleaf: *As the Bonnet Plume
approaches the Peel River, it
broadens and divides into many
channels. The river, however, is
still very fast, frequently clocking
at 10 kph.*

was sheltered from the wind but exposed enough to keep the mosquitoes at bay. We sunbathed, swam, washed, and caught grayling for
our last fish dinner. The water was 13°C. After dinner we climbed to the
top of the cliff to admire the spectacular view up the river through the
canyon and beyond.

Two days later, as the Peel worked its way north, we camped at the
Arctic Circle. The next day we met Neil Colin, a Loucheux Indian from
Fort McPherson, and his son Dempster. We had arranged for them to
take us, our canoes and gear by riverboat over the last, slow 110
kilometres of the Peel. As we motored along, Neil pointed out the
features of the river — the ancient portages and summer fishing camps.
There was some southerners' history, too, the sites where the bodies of
the Lost Patrol had been found. This unfortunate RCMP patrol refused
the help of native guides and lost their way going from Dawson to Fort
McPherson in 1911.

McPherson is a quiet Indian village. We pitched our tents near Neil's
summer camp on the shores of the Peel where the Dempster Highway
ferry crosses the river on its way to Inuvik. When we had finished
dinner and were ready for the sleeping bags, it was 1:00 A.M. and still
light. The husky dogs chained at the camps along the river sang us to
sleep and awoke us again near dawn, when they howled in unison at a
fire siren sounding in the village.

The next morning we stored our rented canoes at Neil's camp; they
would be picked up by the outfitter in Whitehorse. We breakfasted and
packed at a leisurely pace. Bob and Helene decided to hitchhike to
Whitehorse; Shawn and Saundra got a ride on the Dempster-to-Inuvik
with a tourist from Chicago.

Peter and I visited Neil and had coffee. We met his wife Elizabeth,
and sampled some fish he'd smoked; they had been netted in the river.
Elizabeth's mother, Mary, joined us. She made her living through the
hard work of smoke-tanning moosehides. She had been born eighty
years earlier, in the mountains we had canoed through. Neil told us the
Loucheux names of some of the hills, valleys, cliffs, and rivers we had
passed that were nameless on the map. I learned that the Bonnet Plume
is the English translation of an Indian name, and that many Bonnet
Plume families lived in Fort McPherson.

I was wrong in thinking that the river had no history or legends; it
has. But the legends belong to the Loucheux Indians, and the history is

Left: *Early morning sun catches the bright reds and yellows of canoes and canoeists as they break camp for another day's run.*

Below: *End of a journey. The Peel River near Fort McPherson. Buoys mark the top of a whitefish net tended by local Loucheux Indians.*

of their thousands of years of hunting, fishing, and cultural development; not of recent white intruders. Our wilderness was their homeland. Their history may die as the Indians lose their culture — the dog belonging to Neil and Elizabeth's grandson was named Michael Jackson — but this history is still there, though neglected. It is not yet too late for it to be made part of our understanding and knowledge.

I realize that this tale of the Bonnet Plume doesn't have the drama, tension, or excitement of many descriptions of northern river travelling. Partly, I think, this is because some descriptions of pretty uneventful trips are dramatized — "colored" as my friend Eric Morse says — to give them a spurious element of adventure and fearfulness. But there are two other reasons. First, the Bonnet Plume tales we'd heard proved that a wild-river experience can be very difficult for canoeists unfamiliar with reading rapids and white-water manoeuvres. We had the experience and skill to see us through with ease; but more important, we weren't looking for difficulty and adventure. The trip was a chance to get close to nature and to change the pace of our lives; we didn't want excessive stress and pressure. We got what we wanted — two weeks of fabulous scenery and wildlife, excellent canoeing, the company of friends, and a chance to get body, mind, and soul together in the healing northern canoe country.

C.E.S. Franks, author of the classic The Canoe and White Water, *was introduced to river canoeing as an adult. Nowadays, his zeal for white water keeps him busy running spring rivers and has taken him far afield to remote rivers for longer, more fulfilling encounters with the wilderness. He paddled the Bonnet Plume in the summer of 1985. Franks lives in Kingston, Ontario, where he is a member of the Department of Political Studies at Queen's University.*

The South Nahanni River is the centrepiece of Nahanni National Park, which includes 4700 km² of mountains, wild rivers, hot springs and big-game habitat in the southwest corner of the Northwest Territories.

CHAPTER EIGHT

PROTECTED WILD

There is no Canadian wild river that has attracted more interest and attention than the legendary Nahanni. Much of the river is now within the boundaries of a national park. Features such as the 100-metre Virginia Falls, hot springs, tufa mounds, spectacular canyons, and mountain scenery prompted the United Nations Educational, Scientific, and Cultural Organization to designate Nahanni National Park the first World Heritage Site.

Nahanni: River of Gold

BY WALLY SCHABER

T rip notes invariably say something dry like "the headwaters of the South Nahanni River are marked by a pair of shallow lakes at the foot of Mount Wilson." This might make sense in your living room, but when the plane banks to land in the shadow of Wilson, the notes don't come close to what the Nahanni source is really like. The Moose Ponds, as they are affectionately called, seem barely big enough to float a canoe — let alone a plane — but it is here that one of life's very special experiences begins.

The upper Nahanni is a superb wild river. I began guiding canoe trips on the Nahanni in 1976; my rough census indicates that approximately a dozen groups have begun at the Moose Ponds each year since 1981; there was about half that number between 1976 and 1981. Prior to the mid-1970s, only a handful of parties began their canoe journey of discovery right at the source. (After consulting local air charter services and outfitters, you can still find a starting date that will ensure that you have the river all to yourself.)

R.M. Patterson's book, *The Dangerous River,* peaked my interest in the Nahanni. He lived it! I learned from Patterson that all the early prospectors discovered gold — of a sort — on this wild mountain river. I'm convinced that Nahanni riches are not so much in elusive nuggets as in doing, seeing, and being part of a river adventure.

My Nahanni experiences begin with hiking boots, not neoprene socks. I take a lunch and a map to the top of Mount Wilson. Wilson's 1066-metre height above the Moose Ponds translates into a five-hour hike to mountain panorama.

To the north are the snow-capped peaks of the Itse Range along which the Ross River flows. An eight-kilometre portage links this river and the Canol Road with the Moose Ponds, making it a Nahanni access alternative for those with more time and muscle than flight money. A little farther to the north, just off the map and out of sight, are the headwaters of the Bonnet Plume, Keele, and Mountain rivers. Directly east is O'Grady Lake, source of the Natla River. To the west are the Selwyn Mountains that define the Yukon/Northwest Territories border. And to the south, the Nahanni. From Wilson it looks like little more than a meandering creek with tiny patches of white water.

Below Third Canyon and upriver from Second Canyon is Pulpit Rock, a favoured hiking place for Nahanni canoeists. This unusual feature sometimes called "The Gates of the Nahanni" was *formed at an oxbow, when water eroded a straighter path to the sea, leaving a dry channel and a lone spire of rock.*

A single otter floatplane lands
author Schaber and company in
the Moose Ponds. To the south is
majestic Mount Wilson.

The view from Wilson may be seductive, but it is deceptive: people without two or three years of Class III river running should stay atop Wilson! In the seventy kilometres between the Moose Ponds and the junction of the Little Nahanni River, the Nahanni drops 300 metres — a stretch of formidable rapids.

This segment of the Nahanni, dubbed the Rock Garden, is river-running heaven, an experience pristine and personal. It is tempting, however, to rush the river and to run rapids all day, every day. This can be a costly mistake. Time must be taken to assess the variables: the water is cold, the days are long, and canoe loads are at their heaviest. Moreover, you usually have yet to perfect your paddling teamwork, and the most challenging portion of the river is farthest from help. There are plenty of campsites. Everything suggests a slow, relaxed pace and that's exactly how successful parties do it.

Rapids get more difficult as the river progresses. The first day downstream from the Moose Ponds is mostly Class I rapids, although I have had the odd moose or caribou provide a moving obstacle in this section. The second day, tributaries swell the river, making it Class II in dry weather and tricky Class III if it is rainy. During the days 3 and 4 in the Rock Garden, exciting rapids appear in long runs with short pools between. Usually there is just enough time to bail and to congratulate one another. I've often been thankful for ABS plastic canoes that are most forgiving when it comes to sliding around and over the large, rounded boulders.

The Rock Garden has claimed at least one life. In high water, rapids like Initiation, Tributary, Hollywood, and Big Bend, without marked portages, often prove too much for loaded canoes and inexperienced paddlers. Lining is always an option, but I have found it difficult to pinpoint position on 1:250,000 topographic maps (presently the only scale available). I have relied most often on caution and common sense to make it safely down the upper river.

There is no better way to end the rocking and rolling of the upper Nahanni than to languish in a natural hot tub! I think often of lying in the first of three Nahanni hot springs, pushing a floating tray of *hors d'oeuvres* back and forth in the water whilst toasting deeds of skill and daring in the Rock Garden.

Opposite: *Nahanni, the River of Gold, with its prize nugget, Virginia Falls — twice as high as Niagara.*

Below: *Quiet times.*

The Nahanni valley's fabled cliffs
rise above the campsite of a
Nahanni river-runner.

Beneath a spray cover, warmly dressed paddlers concentrate on finding a safe route through the treacherous "Rock Garden."

*Even the roughest, wildest rivers
have stretches of tranquil water.
Here sun and hills are reflected
on the Nahanni.*

Silt-laden waters of Bologna Creek enter the Nahanni below the Rock Garden and begin to cloud the crystal-clear mountain waters of the upper Nahanni. At this point the river is moving along at eight to sixteen kph; with only Class II Elbow rapids to break the ride, you can float eighty kilometres a day on this magic carpet. However, I have always interpreted the silt as a signal that the river valley now has more to say than the river itself.

Below the confluence of the Little Nahanni and the South Nahanni, the entire river can be negotiated by paddlers with only Class I experience. In fact, it is probably more important to be a good hiker than a good paddler for the lower three-quarters of the river.

Hiking is most accessible and enjoyable around the cabin built in the summer of 1978 by newlyweds John and Joanne Moore, as their base for a winter of wilderness living. Their book, *Nahanni Trailhead*, enriches hiking in the area. At their suggestion, I've trekked to alpine meadows high above the river; I've even stumbled on an old horse trail leading back to the Little Nahanni valley.

Down river, sixteen tough kilometres due west, hides the jewel of the Ragged Mountain Range. Shimmering Glacier Lake is surrounded by the highest peaks in the Northwest Territories: MacBrien, Smith, Ida, and Mount Sidney Dobson (2632 metres). There is a meadow at the base of these giants, "The Cirque of the Unclimbables," that is pure magic: sheer granite above, glacier-capped peaks in the distance, opal-green lake below, yesterday's Nahanni valley stretching out of sight to the north and tomorrow's river to the south — and all of this shrouded in wilderness silence.

An hour of drifting from the Glacier Creek campsite brings you to a large yellow sign that announces, "You are now entering Nahanni National Park." This park was established in 1976 to protect the treasures of the Nahanni. The sign means your personal freedom and wilderness experience will be managed to some degree.

How you accept the park and what it stands for depends largely on your philosophy of wilderness preservation. Whatever your feelings, a stop at the park warden's cabin to exchange stories and have a swim in the clear, warm waters of nearby Rabbitkettle Lake is well worthwhile. I always look forward to an invitation from the warden for a guided day trip to Rabbitkettle Hot Springs.

This natural phenomenon is one of the special features that helped the Nahanni gain national-park status. Rabbitkettle Hot Springs figured prominently, too, in UNESCO's designation of the Nahanni region

The "Sluice Box" — one of the
Nahanni's most dangerous
sections of white water.

Below: *Near Glacier Lake, Mt. Harrison Smith towers over a Nahanni hiker.*

Overleaf: *Virginia Falls — one of UNESCO's World Heritage Sites.*

Below: *Near Glacier Lake, Mt. Harrison Smith towers over a Nahanni hiker.*

as a "World Heritage Site" in 1979. The hot springs are so fragile that wardens insist boots be removed when approaching this chalky yellowish-grey structure that stands thirty metres high and sixty metres wide.

"This mound grows at a rate of one-tenth of an inch per year," a warden explains. "You are looking at ten thousand years of nature's handiwork." On tiptoes we climb to a top pool. The 21°C water is crystal clear and slowly overflows in several directions. The warden explains that dissolved minerals, mostly calcium, precipitate and form small terraces that in turn divert the direction of the overflow. In this manner, over centuries, the hot spring has grown to a circular tufa mound. One slip of the foot of a careless bather or enthusiastic photographer could damage a century of nature's labor!

The showpiece of the park is Virginia Falls, Canada's highest. About fifteen kilometres above this impressive, 100-metre cataract, the river slows down and meanders, almost teasing. Closer to the falls, the power of the river becomes dangerously hypnotic. I've stood mesmerized at Sluice Box, a Class VI rapid just above the falls, and imagined enough tongues, eddies, and escape islands to make it through in a canoe. Trouble is, Sluice Box ends in an explosion! Water jets ten to fifteen metres in all directions as if struggling to avoid the brink. A thirty-metre spire of limestone somehow resists all this force and divides the river into a major and minor curtain. There is a treacherous ledge right at water level where the view of the brink is breathtaking. Fortunately, the park people have established a campsite a safe distance away from the falls and have built a boardwalk that guides visitors to many lookout points.

Directly below the falls is Fourth Canyon. Early Nahanni travellers, such as the legendary Albert Faillie and the unfortunate McLeod brothers (found *sans* heads in what is now known as Deadmen Valley), poled and tracked their way upstream for a first view of Virginia Falls. They numbered three canyons below the falls in ascending order. Rolling waves and violent shoreline eddies, combined with sixteen to twenty kph current, make the descent of 7.5 kilometre First Canyon very exciting. When I suggest to most people that they secure their spray skirts for this section of river, I always remember that the prospectors negotiated the river in open skiffs.

Even wilder than Fourth Canyon is Hell's Gate. A stubborn limestone cliff forces the river to take an abrupt left turn, creating two whirlpools with a nasty boil and a ridge of standing waves in the middle. The safest route through is the line of standing waves; but when caution prevails, I've seen paddlers portage along the downstream cliff on a trail that provides excellent canyon viewing.

The Nahanni valley is one of the few areas of Canada to have escaped the effects of the last ice age. Ten thousand years of current have cut a spectacular incision into the Mackenzie Mountains. It's pure heaven floating past the various highlights: Flat River, Third Canyon, Pulpit Rock, Big Bend, Second Canyon, and Deadmen Valley.

If the ill-fated McLeod brothers had not lost their heads, Deadmen Valley could well be called Paradise. The opportunities for exploring, fishing, photography, and relaxation are bountiful. Patterson describes spirited adventures he and his partner had in places such as Prairie Creek, Dry Canyon, Tlogotsho Plateau, and above First Canyon.

First Canyon is the deepest and most spectacular of all. George's Riffle blocks the entrance of this 1000-metre-deep canyon with diagonal, rolling waves and unpredictable haystacks. Many an intrepid voyageur who has not scouted the Riffle has been in for a rough ride and, on occasion, a very cold swim! The walls of First Canyon are marked by dark entrances to craters and caves in the porous limestone. In the 1960s, exploration of one of these caves led to the discovery of nearly 100 Dall's sheep skeletons. The Valerie Caves are now closed to the public to allow for preservation and further study.

But you must concentrate on the water: Lafferty's Riffle is coming up, the last hurrah for the Nahanni traveller before a day's journey brings you to the village of Nahanni Butte, the Liard River, and civilization. Large standing waves bounce happy crews along the outside of the last curve of First Canyon, and then the Nahanni rests.

Memories of last nights on many Nahanni trips include the sun setting over the rim of First Canyon as companions share the last rum rations and soak in a final hot spring. Toasts often echo R.M. Patterson's words, which sum up my feelings for the Nahanni: "The treasure is in the adventure. Let's not destroy the adventure for those who follow by taking the wild out of wilderness."

*Tufa mound at Rabbitkettle Hot
Springs — ten thousand years of
nature's handiwork.*

After long involvement in camp canoeing in Ontario, Wally Schaber founded Black Feather Wilderness Adventures in the early 1970s. Since then, he and his staff have guided thousands of people on expeditions in Canada's premier wild lands. He is as comfortable in Newfoundland as he is on Baffin Island or Kluane, but he is most at home in a canoe, having paddled just about all major Canadian canoe routes. Schaber lives in Ottawa, where he is co-owner of Trail Head, an adventure-sport organization with retail stores in Ottawa and Toronto.

Hiking up Sheaf Creek to the alpine meadows of the Tlogotsho Plateau is a difficult three-to-five-day side trip in the vicinity of First Canyon and Deadman Valley. Ambitious ramblers are rewarded with breathtaking views of the river.

CHAPTER NINE

ONCE WILD

For every river in this nation that has been dammed, there are two or three others — as yet un-dammed — for which develop-ment plans have been drawn. There is not a river in this coun-try of any significance that has not been investigated for its power-generation potential. In rare cases, environmentalists have thwarted damming at-tempts, but more often than not river-preservation advocacy merely shifts development atten-tion to some other nearby river. We need power, but we also des-perately need to consider what is at stake when a river is developed.

Liard: Requiem for a River

BY THOMAS YORK

... I think that the river
Is a strong brown god ... — T.S. ELIOT

The Liard rises in the Yukon. It winds through marshy ground and over sand and gravel bars for 160 kilometres to Liard canyon, eleven kilometres north of the British Columbia border. Then it dips south of the British Columbia/ Yukon border for 240 kilometres before entering the spectacular and dangerous Grand Canyon of the Liard. At the end of this fifty-kilometre chasm, it bends north into the Northwest Territories, where it merges with the Nahanni. Together they flow into the broad Mackenzie at Fort Simpson and into the Arctic Ocean at Inuvik.

Voyageurs, many of whom died in their forties of strangulated hernias from carrying forty-five-kilogram packs, did not like the Liard. It lowered their already low life expectancy. Chief Trader James Anderson wrote in 1851: "You can hardly conceive of the intense horror the men have, to go up to Frances Lake. They invariably on re-hiring endeavour to be exempted from the West Branch. [The Liard was then thought to be the west branch of the Mackenzie.] The number of deaths which have occurred there is fourteen."

Most of these were deaths by drowning. For the Liard, by the time it reaches the Indian village of Lower Post on the British Columbia border, is a strong, broad river — fully as big and swift as the lower Fraser — with rapids as dangerous as the Fraser's Hell's Gate or as Death Rapids on the Columbia used to be, before Micah Dam was built.

The Liard, which means "River of Cottonwoods" (though in 1840 Robert Campbell nicknamed it "River of Malediction"), is still a wilderness river: moose browse in its swales, while hawks and eagles soar high overhead, scanning for prey. Along its tangled cottonwood banks and on its high, red bluffs huge timber wolves and enormous grizzly bears stalk lesser prey — marten, beaver, wapiti — signs of which the wilderness canoeist sees daily.

It was at Lower Post, where the Dease River joins the Liard, that my two sons (ages thirteen and fourteen) and I first sighted the broad, swift, brown Liard in the summer of 1983. We set in at Dease Lake, source of

A solo paddler in the stillness of the dawn.

Left: *An aerial shot of the Liard River, now dammed.*

Opposite above: *Northern beach driftwood.*

Opposite below: *Raindrops hang from the needles of a riverside pine tree.*

the Dease River and the beginning of the arctic watershed, and paddled the 240 kilometres of wilderness river in our five-metre open canoe, for which we had rigged a splash cover.

Rapids on the Dease gave us no occasion to cover our canoe. It was a perfect canoeing river — good current, one small fishing camp, no fellow travellers, no roads, few rapids, which were easily shot, and an abundance of wildlife: moose, black bear, beaver, and porcupine.

Near the confluence of the Dease and the Liard, the current on the Dease quickens to 6.5 kph and a Class III rapid occurs. As the day was hot and retrieval easy, we ran this rapid repeatedly, hoping to capsize and cool off. Finally we just went swimming. Six kilometres downstream the placid Dease pours into the nearly irresistible Liard, though to visit Lower Post on the far bank one must paddle cross-current. When we remarked how hard this was, Don Miller, an old Indian trapper at Lower Post, related how in the summer of 1927 he had watched Albert Johnson, the "Mad Trapper of Rat River," pole upstream on a homemade raft, taking the difficult back way to the Ogilvie/Peel system, from whose Rat River delta he would be flushed and, finally, shot by the Mounties.

After a week on the Dease, which was like a country road compared with the freeway to come, my sons and I felt it would be difficult and hazardous enough to go downstream on the Liard. Don Miller nodded and told us to watch out for Little Canyon, wrongly marked on the maps. He also warned us of numerous unmarked hazards. He was right on all counts. But these were all just names to us, and too many to remember.

. . . a strong brown god — sullen, untamed and intractable . . .

Eighty kilometres downstream we paddled blithely into Little Canyon, thinking ourselves, in a covered canoe that was at tight as a kayak, invulnerable. We were wrong. Skirting the haystacks and massive whirlpool on the right and crashing head-on through the two-metre standing waves on the left, we were in the middle of a maelstrom, drenched by rows of standing waves that rolled over us and our canvas top as over a duck's back. Then suddenly sidewinder waves boiled up from the wake of the whirlpool and we were boxed in: big waves ahead and from the side . . . we were broadside to one or the other; quick as a fish we flipped, and then we were under, struggling to cut the ties and extricate ourselves from our tight-as-a-kayak cover, which had one disadvantage: we couldn't roll the canoe rightside again.

Both boys and I were hanging from the canoe as it wallowed through Little Canyon. Both of them wanted to strike for the shore, but I wasn't sure of the strength of the current and I knew there was another big rapid ahead. My conscious thought was "I might lose one of them," and I wanted to keep them together as long as I could.

Though this was the Liard, not the Columbia, and 1983, not 1968, my mind was immersed in Death Rapids, the time I'd dumped in an open canoe, and went down the hole of the whirlpool; my partner, who didn't go down it, was lost. It was the wake of the whirlpool that saved me.

This time my sons and I managed to get into a back-eddy and out, without loss of life or equipment — everything was tied in and under the cover, but soaked — and we spent the rest of the day drying out. Meanwhile we fished, pulling out one- and two-kilogram dolly varden trout while seagulls screamed and dove at us. This was our only memorable campsite on the Liard. Compared with the rush the river gave, the campsites were dull, a much-needed rest for mind and body, to repair one's courage; for the river, rushing and swishing and roaring past, was ever-present and working, even while we slept. It seemed to taunt, "Come and get me, come and get me, now, while your courage is high," and, had it known about dams and the fate of the Columbia, once wild and untamed, now dammed and diminished, it might have added, "while I am still a great river."

But it was still a great river, and we were still on it. We'd dumped in Little Canyon, which was nothing compared with the three big rapids to come, which were nothing compared with the Grand Canyon of the Liard. We resolved then and there to take out at the Liard River bridge (mile 497 on the Alaska Highway) and not to attempt to run the Grand Canyon. By the time we'd got there, however, the confidence we'd lost at Little Canyon had been restored.

. . . untamed and intractable . . .
Then only a problem confronting the builders of bridges.

The Alaska Highway runs alongside the 320-kilometre stretch of the Liard we were paddling, for the most part right alongside it. But such is the power of the river, the life- and death-giving power of it, that when you are on it you feel totally cut off from all roadways or anything man-

A paddle drips water on the
surface of the quiet river. It is
serene moments such as these
that lure canoeists to wilderness
rivers, as much as the excitement
of running the white water.

made. It is only when you are forced to leave the river, as we were at
Cranberry Rapids, that you punch through the jungle bordering it, your
canoe overhead and a pack on your back, and discover with surprise
that there is a road nearby. Not only is there a road, but on a high bluff
overlooking the rapids are the remains of a burnt-out town, Fireside,
where a few people still live in trailers.

Fireside residents' relationship with the river was as remote as ours
with the highway: they never ventured down to it, and we would not
have struggled up except for the impassable rapids and numerous falls
caused by sedimentary ledges across the river — an obstacle course
unrunnable even by raft. We struck shore in the rain and stumbled over
windfallen corpses of cottonwood tangled with second-growth alder;
we leaped along the bank, canoe and packs on our backs, from sedimentary outcrop to outcrop — a virtually impossible portage.

Finally, we clambered up the hill and resorted to the road, then at
Fireside slid down the steep bluff, the grass wet and slick with sewage,
where in the middle of the wilderness I got a nasty cut from a broken
beer bottle! In heavy rain we left Fireside and Cranberry Rapids and
canoed slowly on to the mouth of the Kechika, where Mountain Portage
Rapids blocked our way. That night we slept the sleep of the dead, in
preparation for the portage the next morning.

This was the hardest portage I have ever done, less than three
kilometres, but it took the whole day. In addition to burnt-over wind-
falls — which had to be walked, balancing a canoe, a metre off the
ground — there were impassible thickets of briar in narrow crevices
between boulders and steep hills and deep ravines. What kept us at it
were occasional glimpses of the alternative: the constricted river break-
ing on boulders and throwing up haystacks three metres high next to
souse holes that issued in boils shooting up with enough force to flip a
canoe. There was not width enough in the turbulence for a whirlpool to
open and close, much less for a canoe to slip through.

The Liard is a big, wild river, untamed and intractable; its banks are a
jungle. Yet remote and unnavigable as it seems to the canoeist, there are
unmistakable bore sites along its shores where drilling has been done to
test the potential of the ground to support a power dam. We had already
passed one such site and we were to pass several more — there are seven
in all; in the Grand Canyon, between Hell's Gate and Devil's Portage
are no less than four, all with a flooding reserve "to 2000 feet contour."
The possibility of damming such a river as this was more than we could

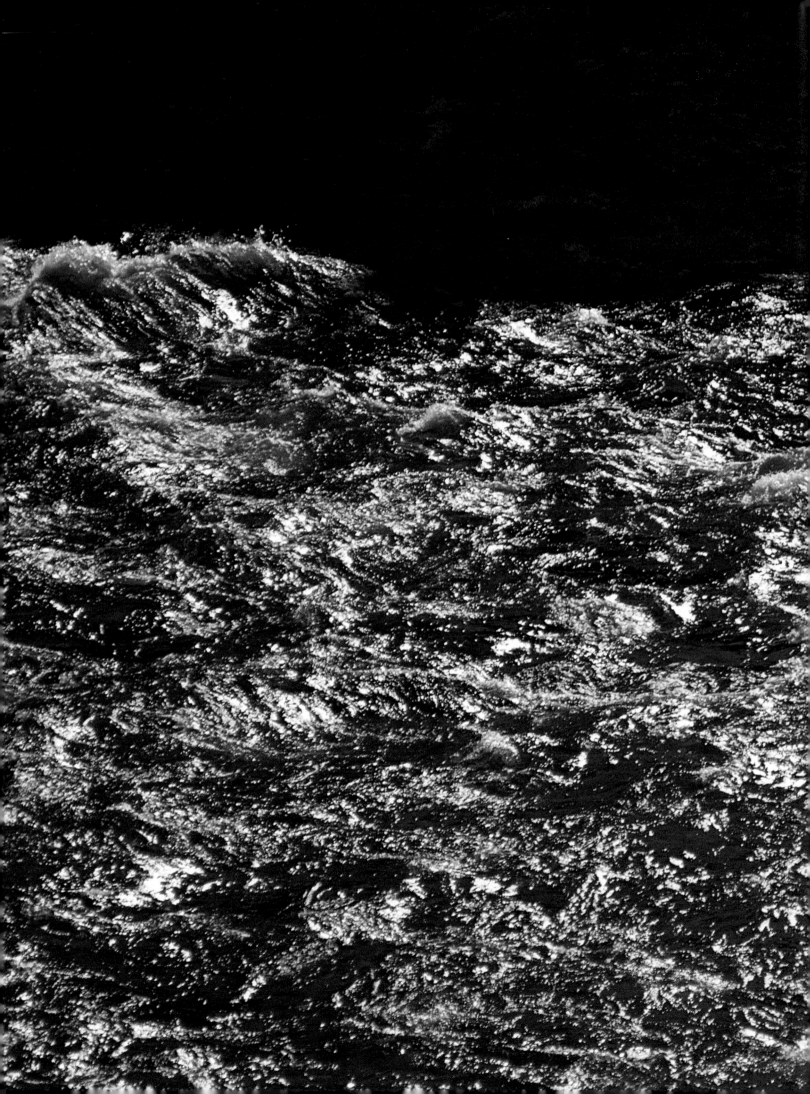

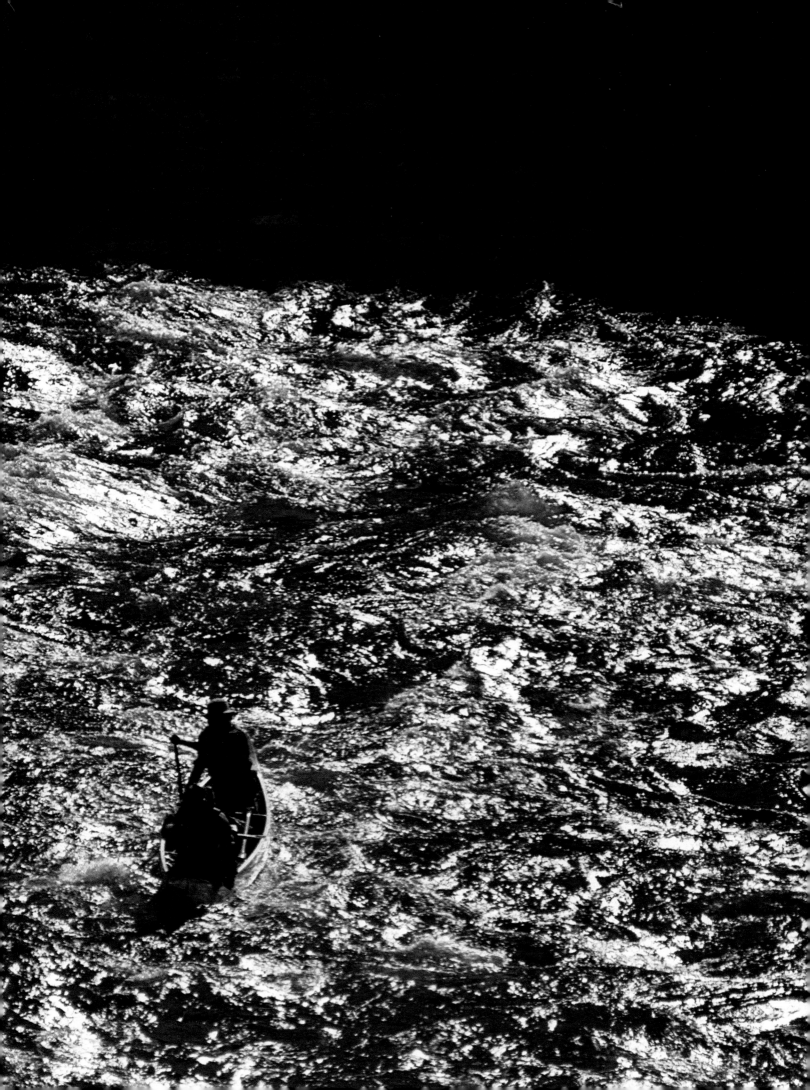

imagine as we slogged and punched our way through the windfallen burn of Mountain Portage Rapids. But as we proceeded downstream to Whirlpool Canyon (where there was neither canyon nor whirlpool), then Portage Brule, a big rapids with a long carry, on our way to the Grand Canyon of the Liard; and as we passed the mouths of more and more rivers — the Rabbit, the Coal, the Smith, the Vents — flowing into the Liard, we began to realize that this river, River of Malediction, River of Cottonwoods, the largest river in northern British Columbia and the southern Yukon, was doomed. Still, it didn't fully come home to us until we met Trapper Ray.

The river is within us, the sea is all about us . . .

He was either drunk or crazy, in fact he was a little of both, when he bore down on us in the Liard River Café, by the bridge at mile 497. We had just ended our trip, but had to wait a few days for our car. We'd looked forward to spending time in the hot springs, where tourists in summer and grizzlies in winter loll and look gaga; but one dip convinced us that it was too hot for comfort — (50°C) — and of discomfort we'd had enough.

Once again, we were wrong. Trapper Ray wanted to shoot the Grand Canyon and wanted me to scout Devil's Gorge with him. So it was that we found ourselves trudging the fifteen-kilometre road he'd swamped out alongside the river, past the flayed wolf's carcass he'd hung from a tree to dissuade trespassers, over beaver dams and through cottonwood brakes, a killing zone for grizzlies. In one tight spot we stumbled on the remains of a horse — decapitated by one swat of a grizzly bear's paw — and Ray warned us to "Look lively now, look lively," and "Stay clear of his little pile of dirt!" I thought this jungle with its mosquitoes and grizzlies more treacherous than the river, but the boys disagreed: they'd take the jungle any day. On we trudged.

At length we reached Trapper Ray's place. He'd built his shack on a high shale cliff dominating the river at a right-angle bend. To the right where the river flowed toward him an alder marsh screened the mud flat where his family of tame beaver lived. Yesterday he had swum with them. His tame pike, Fred, swam there too. To the left the big river, backed by northern spruce forest, gathered momentum as it flowed toward the Grand Canyon of the Liard: a fifty-kilometre stretch of raging white water with an average drop of ten metres per kilometre. If he was going to run it, it would have to be soon. Work at damsite C was slated to commence in the fall. Soon he would look out on a large shapeless lake, his trapline and the road he'd built flooded.

We stayed with Trapper Ray for three days. We overnighted at his stage cabin downstream where the Deer River, a knee-deep trout stream gurgling pleasantly over small stones, splashes into the Liard. We ran the Liard to the beginning of the Grand Canyon, floating downstream with the ease of a morsel into a mouth, which suddenly became the enormous open maw of some mad animal, gleaming with spittle and froth. From atop the 150-metre canyon wall we scouted Devil's Gorge — the ten-metre-high waves, opening and closing eddies and whirlpools, standing waves of two, three, and four metres, and dead ahead the headwall. From that height the waves looked like riffles in cake frosting sliding slowly and majestically in the sun.

Farther downstream raged the Rapids of the Drowned, Surrender Island, Hell's Gate: suicidal rapids all. When at last we left, not having run the canyon, we appreciated Trapper Ray's outlook. Why not go out with one last gesture of defiance? Here where he had made his life and swamped a road through jungle, along this river that for him was home and, from our perspective, paradise . . . all this would soon all be underwater, a huge, shapeless lake "to 2000 feet contour," a swamp.

"Might as well move to Siberia," Ray muttered at the prospect.

Might as well. The winters are no colder there, and the dams are already built.

Thomas York grew up in Little Rock, Arkansas, and attended Tulane University in New Orleans, finishing his studies with a Ph.D. in English literature. He immigrated to Canada in 1962, studied theology at the University of Toronto, and took a passionate interest in the north, travelling many routes by canoe, including two trips across the Arctic from Yellowknife to Baker Lake. He has written a number of novels set in the Canadian north, including Snowman *(Doubleday, 1976),* Trapper *(Doubleday, 1981; rpt. Avon, 1983), and* The Muskox Passion *(Doubleday, 1978), which won the Mark Twain Best Comic Novel of the Year Award. York, who is an ordained minister of the United Church of Canada, became a Canadian citizen in 1970 and lives in Waterloo, Ontario, where he is Chaplain to the University of Waterloo and Wilfrid Laurier University.*

Quotations from "The Dry Salvages," The Four Quartets *by T.S. Eliot in* Collected Poems, 1909-1962, *published by Faber and Faber, 1963.*